Circle Your Wagons

Journey to
My Empowered Self

Abbi K. Harrington

Nancy,
Shine your light brightly!
Love,
Abbi

Circle Your Wagons
Journey to My Empowered Self

ISBN-13: 978-1-7374553-3-2

Although the author and publisher have made every effort to ensure that the information in this book was correct at press time, the author and publisher do not assume and hereby disclaim any liability to any party for any loss, damage, or disruption caused by errors or omissions, whether such errors or omissions result from negligence, accident, or any other cause.

Printed in the United States of America.

This is the recipe of life
Said my mother
As she held me in her arms as I wept
Think of the flowers you plant
In the garden each year
They will teach you that people too
Fall ... root ... rise
In order to bloom

~Rupi Kaur

Dedication

Toni Morrison once said, "A sister is someone who can be seen as both ourselves and very much not ourselves --a special kind of double." To this I would respectfully add, "… a special kind of double trouble." The collective energy of sisters can move mountains; it can also cause the men in the room to turn and run the other way, so watch out and move over, because here we come!

Navigating this life without my sisters would have been impossible. They have always honored me in the most divine way, and I am returning the favor by dedicating this book to each of their sweet, loving, souls. Thank you, Terri, Heidi, and Jenni, for shining so brightly in my life. Here's to the warriors we truly are!

And how can I not include all the other strong women I am surrounded by? My son's birth mom, Shaneka, who's strength and courage is an inspiration to me. From those who came before me, like my grandmother, Eunice Harrington, to my precious nieces, Meghan, Erin, Sarah, and Jessi – I'm honored to watch you lead with love and compassion. These are your gifts to share with your loved ones and the world.

I would be remiss if I didn't give special recognition to the woman who made all of this possible, my dear, sweet momma, Karen Rauch Harrington. She nurtured my sisters and me and provided for our needs in the best way she knew. It had to be a monumental task, for sure. I am forever grateful to her kind and gentle soul. I love you, Momma!!

Table of Contents

Introduction

"Wouldn't it be wonderful if we could be spared from all suffering? No, it wouldn't. We would not evolve as human beings and would remain shallow, identified with the external form of things. Suffering drives us deeper."

~Eckhart Tolle

I had a moment of amazing clarity a few years ago while spending time at a monastery to quietly reflect on my life. It was a cold, rainy day, and I was warming myself by the fireplace in the library when I randomly looked up and saw a book titled *Angel of Protection*. Actually, it wasn't so much that I saw it as that it *jumped out* at me. I stood, pulled it off the shelf, and opened it to a story about Archangel Michael who had stepped in to protect children from their cruel father. It couldn't have become any clearer to me that my family had guardian angels watching over us, keeping us safe and protected. Instantly, I was willing to trust, once again, the message the Universe had been trying to tell me all my life: that everything would be okay.

My intention for writing this book was to share the history of the Harrington family and pass on an insightful legacy to the younger generations. I also wanted to share my journey of awakening with others who may have had similar family experiences and are looking for opportunities for transformation. My hope is that I can shed some light on why life sometimes feels like one struggle after another, rather than something we can embrace and enjoy. Most of all, I want the reader to know that it's never too late. I have come to understand that we are all right on time!

I grew up on a fifth-generation family farm in Nebraska during the 1960s and '70s. I was the third daughter born to Tom and Karen Harrington within a span of three years, with my baby sister joining us four years later. My father's life had taken a drastic turn when at the age of nineteen his own father passed away in a tragic car accident. Dad, who had been away at college, had to come home and begin his career in farming. After a few years of bachelorhood, he met my mother, and they married a short time later.

For Mom, who had been raised in a city, farm life was an enormous adjustment. Add three daughters and an emotionally needy husband to the picture, and it had to have been challenging for her. Whatever energy she had left after caring for three toddlers, Dad sucked it right out of her! As you can imagine, some pretty unhealthy patterns, some of them passed down from previous generations, continued as our family grew.

A turning point in my own journey, and part of the inspiration for this book, came when I realized that I had grown up in a family system where the children took on roles usually held by adults. This is common when there is unresolved trauma and unmet emotional needs – someone always has to step in to keep the family functioning. My oldest sister Terri, for example, saw that our mom and dad were in crisis a good share of the time and was determined from a young age to "save the parents and the children."

Being the sensitive middle child, I perceived my mother's sadness and as a young girl made the unconscious decision to hold her sorrow in my body. I felt like I cried for half my life, never realizing that much of the sadness wasn't even mine. I was like a sponge, soaking up many emotions that my family members weren't able to deal with. While it may have been kind of me, it most certainly wasn't kind *to* me. I would have to journey through many dark times before I found the authentic Abbi, the one I'd hidden away in order to survive growing up. It would take me many years to realize that my family system was also perfect for teaching me the lessons I've come here to learn in this lifetime.

While my primary purpose has been to awaken to my true self, I've also felt called to help others who have lived with similar family dynamics – those of codependency and enmeshment. In her article "No Boundaries: Breaking Codependence," *Experience Life* contributor Jill Metzler Patton describes codependent families as those in which members develop maladaptive behaviors to cope with each other's unprocessed emotional pain.

"Codependency," writes Patton, "is a willingness to adapt to others' needs, a selfless desire to help."

Codependency is also seen as an abandonment of the self. When a child's needs and emotions are punished or ignored by the adults in their life, low self-esteem and shame likely develop. They lose the connection to their innate self because their thoughts and behaviors revolve around others and whatever issue they are experiencing.

It is easy to see why such a dynamic has historically been the norm for farm families. Given the fickleness of Mother Nature and other variables, farming was, and is, one of the riskiest business ventures, and one of the most dangerous professions. The only objective of the first generations was survival, which meant not losing the farm, no matter what the cost. According to a growing body of research in the field of genetics, many of the codependent behaviors would have unconsciously been passed down from one generation to the next.

That said, the way the "survival genes" manifest is unique to each family. In our case, we had at the helm, a man who had been plunked down on a farm with very little knowledge of farming. Although my father was a risk-taker, innovative, intelligent, and eccentric; he was also, at times, very reckless and cruel. These traits, coupled with his anger and sadness over his fate, resulted in a chaotic environment that was very difficult to navigate, particularly for a child. I am living proof that it is possible to overcome the effects of living within such a family system. To do so, it is necessary to learn how to set healthy boundaries and communicate honestly with family members.

I am forever grateful for this journey and all that it continues to teach me on a daily basis. I have a deep knowing that the outcome is one of peace, love, and joy. Above all else, awakening to your higher self involves learning to embody self-love on a deep level. Self-love is the greatest gift we can give to ourselves as human beings.

If there is one message I would like the reader to take away from my story it is that there is always a path to freedom and a life of inner happiness. No matter how many limiting beliefs an individual might be holding onto from their past, those beliefs can be transmuted and transformed. The resources are everywhere, and it basically comes down to our willingness, courage, and sometimes the assistance of a professional coach to learn to transform what's not working for you. There will be days when you will want to quit, I promise you. I encourage you to stay the course and on those days be extra gentle and love yourself right where you are.

It truly does take a commitment to awaken to and accept your loving, beautiful self, and I hope you are up for it, because it's worth every gold star in the vast Universe!

> *"Self-love is the honor, reverence and compassion respecting all the Divinity and all the Humanness that is you."*
>
> **~Donna Bond**

PART 1

Circle Your Wagons

Guardian Angels

The wind is singing in the trees,
The stars are shining with the breeze,
An owl is looking at me all night long.

~Abbi, age 8

As a precious young girl growing up on the farm, I would, every once in a while, find myself alone with my father and contemplating my death because of his extreme recklessness and lack of consideration for me around the equipment and animals. I can remember, as far back as age four, being so puzzled and confused that he would even consider putting me in such dangerous predicaments time and time again.

I could sense that a situation felt dangerous because of how scared I felt inside my body, with butterflies in my stomach and a pounding heart inside my chest.

What I didn't have was the voice to say, "No, I don't want to ride in the back of your stupid pickup with your crazy driving! You scare me, Daddy."

I trusted him because that's what I was supposed to do, right? Yet I can vividly remember thinking over and over, *"My daddy loves me, why is he trying to kill me?"*

My father also exhibited inconsiderate behavior inside the house. He was not there very often – mostly it was for meals and to sleep; otherwise, he was outside working on the farm. When he was with us, he wasn't really present. I vividly remember him, sitting next to us in his white tee shirt and underwear, attempting to read bedtime stories. He would skip pages, and after about five minutes his voice would start to trail off because he didn't want to read anymore.

In frustration, I'd grab the corner of the book and turn back to the right page and proclaim, "Dad, we are on this page!"

He'd only read for a little bit longer before he started skipping pages again, and if I threw a fit, he'd throw the book in the air and command, "Get out of here and leave me alone, you bratty kids!"

I went to bed rather distraught on those occasions.

One hot, dry, windy day in my fifth summer, I found myself standing in the dirt scoop attached to the back of my dad's tractor. We were four miles from home, and he was driving, going as fast as the tractor would go, down the gravel road. The dirt scoop was a metal box, approximately eight feet wide and ten feet long. It had a hydraulic arm that allowed the box to open, and a sharp edge that allowed dirt to be peeled up and loaded into the box as the tractor moved forward. When the box was full of dirt the hydraulic arm would close so you could unload it at a different location. It reminded me of the open mouth of a shark, and if you were in the way when the mouth closed that would be the end of you!

I stood in the scoop, the bottom was open about ten inches, watching the road whiz past right underneath my feet. I was also holding on for dear life, petrified that I might fall out or the scoop might close on me and crush me. All of a sudden, I detected another occupant riding along with me – a spider – and decided that if Dad's behavior didn't kill me, the spider would. I watched that spider like a hawk, my eyes darting back and forth from the gravel road right under my feet back to its furry body, with a rhythm that suggested panic. I remember having an intense headache, a parched mouth, and a terrible ache in my stomach (that would remain for many years) as I stood gripping the side of the scoop with all my might. All I wanted was to make it back home safely to my mother.

I also desperately wanted to scream and cry, "Get me out of here!" but at five years young I already knew that when I was with my dad, I had to keep my mouth shut. He hated seeing me cry, and he certainly didn't place value on anything I had to say.

Luckily, I did make it back to Mom that day, but oh, what horrifying shape I was in: crying and dirt-covered with my hair all tangled. I assume I was thirsty, hungry and exhausted, but glad to be home. Like many times during my childhood, at some point I left my body because the intensity of my fear was way beyond my capacity to process, or even feel.

I have a difficult time imagining how our mother trusted us with Dad, but I certainly understand why she needed the break. She had three young girls, and by this time my baby sister had joined the family as well. Besides, it wasn't uncommon for young children to tag along with their fathers on the farm, though I highly doubt other dads would put their little girl in a dirt scoop and drive with her standing in it.

As for the spider, I cannot be sure it was really in the dirt scoop; in fact, it now seems rather unlikely. Yet, real or imagined, I do have a very clear memory of it. At age five, I had a vivid imagination, laced with lots of "worst-case scenario" scenes. Possibly the spider was a message from Spirit, telling me I was protected during that hellish ride. What I have come to know and understand after surviving my childhood is that my family was totally and completely covered by the loving wings of a host of angels. They protected all of us from the negligent, often reckless ways in which my father chose to live, and the danger he brought to our doorstep. The poem I wrote about an "owl watching over me" all night long speaks very clearly to my knowing that I was protected and cared for by a force far greater than my parents.

That knowing was further validated during my experience at the monastery I mentioned earlier. I know it was no accident, but a nudge from Spirit that prompted me to turn my head and look up at *Archangel Michael: Angel of Protection.* It was the word *protection* that locked my eyes on the book. I reached up to pull it off the shelf, and as I was randomly thumbing through, I stopped at a page that said something to the effect of, "It is a bad thing when a father mistreats his children." It was Archangel Michael's job to protect these precious lives. I left the monastery amazed by the synchronicity, how Spirit had met me in that room on that day and directed me to that book. I still draw on that memory during those times when I'm struggling with trust and require some reassurance from the Universe, from God.

There was always a lot of chaos whenever Dad interacted with the farm animals, yet in the end my sisters and I were always spared from harm. One cool, damp, and cloudy fall day, my sister Heidi and I were outside with him while he was trying to sort and move cows to a different field. When the cows didn't cooperate on this particular day – some ran in the wrong direction – he responded by throwing cement chunks at them and tried to stab them with a fence post.

"You goddamn sons of bitches," he yelled, "Heya, git going!"

When that failed, he then turned his frustration on me and Heidi, no matter that we were only five and six years old.

"What in the hell are you doing?" he yelled at us, "Get over here!"

Even at that tender age, I knew he was acting foolishly, and my heart was broken for the cattle he mistreated because of his frustration.

Eventually, Dad did somehow succeed in getting the cows where they needed to be. Then, for reasons I'll never understand, he decided to put Heidi and me on two humongous and rather wild horses; this despite the fact that we had never ridden before, and that the horses were wound up from all the craziness of sorting the rebellious bovines.

I am positive I did not want to ride that day, just as I'm certain the horses sensed my nervousness. As soon as we were placed on their backs, they took off galloping toward the driveway, with Heidi and me holding on for dear life and screaming at the top of our lungs. What I remember most, though, was that all-too-familiar feeling of, "I gotta stay alive."

Suddenly, and thank God for our sakes, the horses decided they'd had enough of our screaming and bucked us off right in front of our house. The move was in unison, as if choreographed, but it was far from smooth. I jumped up unscathed and ran with my sister away from those wild, overgrown, snorting beasts! My memory gets fuzzy here, but I'm sure I was crying hysterically as Heidi led me to the house to find Mom and hopefully, some comfort.

Knowing Heidi, she chalked it up to a hell of an experience and was not shaken one bit! In fact, when I asked her recently what she remembered about this episode, she replied, "I know I loved horses, so I was probably happy to ride one that day."

Feeding the cows was another terrifying experience. Dad and I would go out in the truck and drive along the terraces, which were three-foot, grass-covered, "steps" cut into the side hill of the pasture to help prevent erosion. He'd put the truck in low gear, then hop out and go sit on the back end, dumping protein pellets while the cows followed.

As the truck steered itself, I'd sit helplessly in the passenger seat, staring wide-eyed ahead and yelling, "Dad! We are going to fall down the terrace!"

He would just laugh and call out, "You are such a chicken shit!"

It would have been easy enough for him to teach me to steer the truck away from the edge of the terraces, but my guess is that he got a perverse thrill from my fear.

For Dad's fortieth birthday his friends delivered a smelly, obnoxious, overly friendly billy goat to our front door. What was meant as a joke turned into another heartbreaking situation. My dad tied the goat up to a post at the end of the driveway, hoping to keep it away from our house because the stench was unbearable. The goat repeatedly broke free and one day he got loose and ran up the driveway alongside my sister Jenni. At the time she was terrified because she thought the goat was chasing her, but later she realized he was just being playful.

After that, Dad did everything to get rid of the goat, including shooting at it and clubbing it with a golf club and two-by-fours. As much as I was afraid of the goat, I was horrified by how my father treated it. Finally, our dear neighbor came and asked if she could take it to her farm and I couldn't have been happier. That billy goat lived happily ever after, though with PTSD, I'm certain. After the goat episode I was told to go out and pick up all the things my dad had beaten the goat with, as if that could somehow erase what had happened. Why he just hadn't loaded it up and returned it to his friend is beyond me.

All I ever wanted as a child of Tom and Karen Harrington was to be loved, nurtured, and cared for. As a mature adult, I realize each had their own set of unresolved childhood issues that made it impossible for them to love me unconditionally. When I was about eight years old my dad gave me the nickname "Shorty," which was actually kind of fitting because I was small-framed. At the time I remember thinking that maybe he did love me. I felt quite proud and important too, like, "Hey, Dad noticed me, he's given me a special name!"

I had also earned another nickname from my mom and my second-grade teacher: "worry wart." I would cry every day when school ended because I was afraid the bus would leave without me and I wouldn't make it home. I didn't trust that anyone was looking out for my welfare or would even notice if I wasn't on the bus. That nickname stuck for several years, and though I hated it I could never summon the nerve to tell my mom how it felt.

Worry was the great equalizer for me; it gave me some feeling of control in a world where I felt powerless. I never knew from one day to the next what harrowing experience my older sisters and I would face. On one occasion, Dad commanded me, Terri, and Heidi to go down to the bull pen and pick up the corrugated sheet metal that had blown off the shed during a recent windstorm.

"But Dad," Terri piped up, "what if the bulls chase us?"

"Those bulls won't bother you – now, goddamn it, get down there!" Dad bellowed.

Knowing we had no choice, the three of us resignedly trudged down to the pen where the bulls awaited. Dad owned a herd of Charolais cattle, a breed that originated in France. They are a fair amount larger than those of other common breeds, such as Hereford and Angus, that most farmers in the area raised. The bulls, which can easily weigh two thousand pounds, are very squirrely by nature and cannot be trusted around people they are not familiar with.

Once inside the pen, my sisters and I took hold of the large, rather cumbersome pieces of sheet metal and slowly began dragging them across the muddy lot, careful not to cut our fingers on the sharp edges. Suddenly, the tinny, drumming noise they made turned to thunder, and when we looked back there were a couple of mighty fine Charolais bulls running after us with eyes bulging, hind legs bucking in the air, and heads down and butting. It was rodeo time, and we were their targets!

"Run!" Terri screamed at the top of her lungs, "Run! The bulls are coming!"

Overcome with fear and excitement, we began running as fast as we could through the mud in our heavy boots. It took several steps before I realized I was still dragging the piece of metal and let it drop to the ground. By the grace of God and adrenaline pumping through our bodies, the three of us high-jumped the five-foot-tall wooden fence and landed face-down in the mud on the other side. Gasping for air, Terri and I looked at each other and burst out laughing, while Heidi just got up and walked off. She was mad as hell at Dad for ordering us to get in the pen with the bulls.

"What the hell was that all about?" Terri exclaimed. "Why did he make us do that?"

There were very few experiences on the farm that made me laugh, but for some reason this unexpected bullfighting event was one of them. Possibly I was beginning to understand that we girls could survive anything Dad put us up to. I have the sense now that this was what he was trying to instill in us all along.

We had some pretty major snow blizzards during the '70s that would keep us housebound for a week at a time. No school meant more work around the farm, and priority number one was helping Dad rescue the baby calves who had no shelter. Most farmers had either a barn or some type of shed available for the calves during a blizzard, but not us. We'd have to pick up the calves and carry them a good distance to the heated shop where they'd stay until the storm passed; then we'd carry them back to the momma cows. Even then, it was evident to me that Dad was addicted to stress and drama, as he was always creating it!

Other times, he would make me go with him to the pasture to help vaccinate the new calves. We would head into the pasture, Dad carrying an eight-foot-long metal rod with a hook on one end, and me following with the bucket of medicine and syringes. His homemade "calf catcher" allowed him to sneak up behind the calf and hook its back leg and I was always amazed at his accuracy and success. We would then wrestle the calf to the ground so Dad could administer the vaccinations. We wore no protective gear, and there were many times when I feared for Dad's safety as well as my own. It seemed no matter how hard I tried I was always in harm's way. He repeatedly chose to put me and my sisters there, until we were forced to learn how to keep ourselves safe.

For years, that word – safe – was a loaded one for me; it triggered all my rage and fury at having the "safe" scared out of me for so long. (Even today, I feel a twinge every time I hear "Stay *safe*"; "Travel *safe*"; "Be *safe*," which of course is being bandied about even more during the pandemic.) How do you build trust when the adults you call Mommy and Daddy are oblivious to your wellbeing and your feelings of fear?

My trusting of a power greater than myself continues to be a work in progress. Through the years I have leaned on God during difficult times, only to allow my ego to take over again and run the show when things were running smoothly. Having a father who didn't believe in any power other than his own, I learned to do life alone, without support from my Higher Power. I'd like to believe that I finally get it and realize how beautiful life is with the energy of the Divine Love walking alongside me. I also know that I need to nourish its presence by becoming still and listening. It is a daily practice.

CHAPTER 2

Centennial Hill Farm

On the eighth day,
God looked down on his planned paradise and said,
"I need a caretaker." So God made a farmer.

~Paul Harvey

Our family farm was homesteaded by my great-great-grandparents, Thomas and Mary Barber, in 1867, after they immigrated from England to York County, Nebraska. In 1873, Thomas established a Timber Claim Right on the land, which meant he was entitled to ownership because he had planted a certain number of trees on the property. He also purchased land from the Union Pacific Railroad in 1876, one hundred years after our country's birth, hence the name "Centennial Hill Farm." The signage is still visible on the farm shed today, six generations of Harringtons later! Thomas Barber's oldest daughter, Lela, married Harry Harrington, and they took over the farm after Lela's parents retired to Long Beach, California.

The farm was lost during the Depression years, but my grandparents, Wayne (Lela's oldest son) and Eunice Harrington, bought the farm back in 1939 when my father was a young boy of six. My grandparents made many improvements on the land, including digging irrigation wells, leveling the land, building a shop, hog house, and grain storage facilities. My grandfather also owned and operated a truck stop in Fairmont, Nebraska that included a gas station, restaurant, cabins, and a mechanic shop for his fleet of trucks that hauled salt and grain. Here's a fun family secret I learned from people who knew my grandfather: during the Prohibition, when the trucks went to Kansas for a load of salt, they would hide alcohol underneath the salt and bring it back to Nebraska. Another story was that Grandfather Wayne, who was also a pilot, lost his license after flying his plane through the underpass at Fairmont. Indeed, learning about my grandfather gave me a glimpse into where my father had gotten some of his eccentric behaviors.

Dad was an only child, and likely a lonely one, as his parents were very busy tending to their truck stop and newly purchased farm. The story goes that Dad used to stand on a box to play pool with the truck drivers at the truck stop, and learned to hold his own quite well. Bets were often placed on the games he played, and the regulars sought to line their own pockets by pairing Dad up with unsuspecting truck drivers passing through. He never failed to clean their pockets.

This was where Dad learned, at a very young age, the colorful language that would pepper his conversations for the rest of his life. I think it was his way of expressing the deep-seated emotions he was so out of touch with. He also used profanity to scare or motivate those around him, with no human or animal spared, including his four daughters.

Dad was an inquisitive child with an adventurous spirit, which made it difficult for him to sit behind a school desk all day and follow the teacher's instructions. He struggled through elementary and middle school in York, Nebraska, after which my grandparents sent him to Shattuck Military School in Faribault, Minnesota. In my opinion, this was probably a wise decision, as running their businesses seemed to take precedence over actively parenting their only child. Though I wasn't there, I can imagine Dad grew up with an emotional void, as any child would when their parents aren't able to provide the love and attention they need to flourish.

My sister Jenni told me that she once randomly asked him, "Dad, did your dad love you?"

After thinking for a bit, he replied, "He was proud of my athletic abilities."

Jenni pressed further. "But did he love you?"

My father couldn't answer, and Jenni remembers leaving the room astounded and sad.

With me, Dad was more forthcoming, saying more than once that he felt like he had a "hole in his soul."

Though he sorely missed his parents and grandparents, Dad thrived at Shattuck, where strict rules and solid boundaries replaced the lack of structure he was used to at home. While there he discovered his many athletic talents, and excelled in football, basketball, and tennis. He was required to write to his parents every week and in his letters, he routinely talked of trying to get his grades up, the number of demerits he had, and his "perfect record" at chapel – he fell asleep every time he attended! He was quite proud of that. It also appeared in his letters that he was desperately trying to get his parents' attention. His participation in sports earned him a lot of positive attention from adults, and he remained passionate about them for most of his adult life.

In one letter, written shortly after basketball season had ended, he lamented to his parents, "Now that basketball is over there's nothing to look forward to. There's no nervous feeling in my stomach and I miss it a lot."

He was apparently much less fond of tennis, complaining in a letter that "it doesn't do anything but give me a backache."

Shattuck was five hundred miles from the farm, which meant his parents weren't able to attend very many of his athletic competitions. When he knew they were coming, the excitement in Dad's letters was palpable. He also talked of his eventual return to Nebraska.

"I have been learning to juggle with four balls," he wrote, "so when I get home I can throw those dishes around like a madman. Ha. This morning I juggled eggs and I didn't break them!"

For sure my father had a mischievous streak, as evidenced by the story he used to tell us girls of the time he and his classmates filled the bottom of the fire escape with water and allowed it to freeze.

The next day at breakfast Dad yelled, "Fire!" and one of his schoolmates slid down the fire escape, where he promptly slipped on the ice and broke his leg.

From time to time he proudly shared this and other military school antics, which he considered clever. Sometimes something as simple as breakfast could trigger a fond memory.

My sisters and I would be sitting around the table with him and he'd hold up the toast he was buttering and say, "This kid I went to school with named Fred had frizzy hair. It looked hideous and bugged me, so I'd butter some toast and slap it on top of his head and squish it into his hair."

I'm sure I looked at Dad and wondered how he could be so cruel. I distinctly remember feeling sad for the young man on the receiving end of his antics.

He also took great satisfaction in breaking Shattuck's rules. In one letter he reported, "Last night the whole school went over to St. Mary's (a girls' school) to see some geeks sing some ballads, so Richard and I went downtown to see a good show and we didn't get caught either. Had a good time for once."

His letters were once again filled with excitement as graduation neared. He was making all kinds of plans for where his parents would stay when they arrived in Faribault for the ceremony, as well as the trips he was going to take after graduation.

Of course, there was his usual mischievousness. "I'll put a note in my graduation announcements: Don't come but send a gift."

I can just imagine my grandmother offering her typical response: "Oh now, Tommy!"

Dad spent that summer after graduation helping on the farm, and in August, he reported to the Husker football training camp at Curtis, Nebraska.

An article in the local newspaper stated, "Harrington, a six-footer, who tips the beams at 183 pounds, is a candidate for an end position."

Tragedy struck in February of 1952, when Dad was a freshman at University of Nebraska – Lincoln. His father was driving down an icy highway when he lost control of his truck and slid into a ditch, colliding head-on with a tree. He suffered severe injuries and died a few days later. He had lost his hand in a combine accident during harvest the previous fall, which had no doubt been extremely difficult for a man as active, and as prominent in the community, as my grandfather. I'd also bet that trying to navigate the slippery highway with one hand possibly led to his demise.

In the blink of an eye, any plans my nineteen-year-old father had for his future were destroyed. He had to leave UNL and come back to the farm, where he was expected to fill some mighty big shoes! His mother offered whatever support she could and assisted him with the financial aspect of the business. Eventually, and after making lots of mistakes, he did manage to build a Hereford cattle herd, and raise corn, wheat, and milo quite successfully.

Four years later he married Mom, who he had met on the tennis courts when she was a student at UNL. Little did either of them realize that they were about to exchange the game of "love" and "deuce" for a very fast-paced and frantic game of life. I don't think my mother had any clue what she was in for; she was desperate to spread her wings and leave home, as she and her own mother didn't have the most congenial relationship.

CHAPTER 3

Harrington and Girls

"Fathers, be good to your daughters.
You are the God and the weight of her world."

~John Mayer

And so it came to be that a would-be college football star and his young, innocent bride stood at the helm of his inherited farm west of Benedict, Nebraska. Having three daughters in less than three years only added to Dad's considerable stress. Little girls weren't much use on a farm, especially one that was already short on laborers, and I've no doubt he was often left wondering how he was going to handle all that fate had dealt him.

In time, Dad seemed to settle into a life of unpredictability that the farming industry has always been known for, and a habit of eagerly creating chaos to garner attention. As for my mother, she became entrenched in her role as the caretaker and nurturer of all Dad's whims and needs. The most enduring memory I have of my parents' relationship was how extremely critical my dad was of my mother, no matter what she was doing or not doing.

To this day, I can recall his whiny voice saying, "Karen, why are you trying to plant flowers there?" or "Karen, why are you cooking again? Can't you come and sit down?" My mother seldom fought back. She would just stop what she was doing and do as dad commanded. As soon as he left the house, she would go back to whatever activity he had interrupted.

Though she took the path of least resistance, my mother was one of the strongest women I've ever known. Marriage to my father was not a pleasant experience a good share of the time, yet she managed to maintain a sense of self, despite his efforts, unconscious as they were, to emotionally and mentally destroy her. She also made sure we got the hell off the farm, and away from him, as much as possible. We went to Sunday school and church, were involved in 4-H, played softball, visited our grandparents frequently and took swimming lessons. She hired high school girls to chauffeur us to all the activities.

Mom was an excellent cook and became well-known for her delectable meals. Food was more than sustenance to her; it was her love language. She also kept a very tidy home, nurtured an amazing fruit and vegetable garden, and kept a well-manicured yard laced with beautiful flowers – skills she would pass to her four daughters and her grandchildren as well. Mom also cultivated a full social and civic life, becoming involved with everything from church boards to bridge clubs and more.

As we grew up my sisters and I also settled into what would be our family roles. Terri, the oldest, played the "matriarch," which as I stated earlier, she described as, "Save the parents, save the children, and get out of there!" And get out of there she did, the day after she graduated from high school. I vividly remember the whole family crying when she headed to UNL, only to return for weekend visits and holidays. Terri's departure was indeed a blow, for if anyone served as the competent adult in our family dynamic, it was her. Heidi, who was thirteen months her junior, was tough, stubborn, and couldn't be shaken. Dad could always depend on her for help on the farm as she preferred that to helping Mom around the house. She also was, and still is, my rock. Eleven months after Heidi was born, I joined the tribe. I was the tender-hearted, quiet one. Terri used to introduce me by saying, "That's Abbi, she's shy," as if to prepare the person I was meeting for any awkwardness.

Our baby sister Jenni, who came along four years after me, has always claimed that she had different parents than we did, or at least a different dad. She was rarely included in any of the farm jobs, or the treacherous obstacle courses Dad seemed to have designed specifically for the three of us. That is not to say that she doesn't have the same strong work ethic; in fact, she is one of the hardest working women I know. To anyone outside our family, the Harrington tribe appeared to be a well-oiled machine: Dad ran the show, the girls did what he commanded to the best of their abilities, and life was good, or so it seemed.

Growing up, Heidi and I spent a lot of time playing house in the shelterbelts – the rows of trees often planted around the edges of the fields to block the wind and stop the soil from eroding. Looking back, those experiences were vital to my mental and emotional health. How very magical it was! How protected and free I felt! Just being amongst the trees helped to heal some of my very early trauma.

Instinctively we knew when it was time to get on our bikes and travel the half-mile home for lunch. We also had the sense, like Jack in the Beanstalk, to tiptoe past the "sleeping giant" (aka Dad), so as not to get caught by him. We made sure to leave before he woke up from his nap; otherwise, he'd come up with some ridiculous job out in the field such as standing corn up that had been covered up with dirt from the cultivator or planting corn seeds by hand because the planter boxes were plugged and had stopped putting seeds into the ground. Dad didn't like looking out over his field and seeing blank spots where there was supposed to be corn growing. That's where the three able bodied daughters came into play.

I was about eight years old when those shenanigans started, and I'll tell you what: I still remember how I felt as Dad drove us to the middle of the field (which was a few miles from home), dumped us out the back of his pickup, and left. It wouldn't be long before the worry set in. Was he ever going to come back and get us? And why couldn't he stay and help us with the work? It left me feeling alone and abandoned.

Was I crazy for thinking he should be helping us? No, I don't think so. All I could see for miles were acres and acres of cornfields, with a monumental task at hand and no responsible adult to guide us.

When he did come and get us, he would usually be in a hurry, telling us to hop in the back of the pickup even though our work wasn't done. We'd never go back and finish it either, which made me feel like he was just being cruel and invented absurd jobs to see if he could take us down. Though I didn't think about it consciously at the time, there was no way I was going to allow him to do that. I guess you'd call it resiliency. On those nights I'd lay awake wondering if we would have to go back the next day, but I never brought it up for fear of tempting him.

On the worst of summer days, Dad would order us to go to the fields with corn knives to chop the weeds out of soybean fields. Staring out at the 160 acres of soybeans we had to cover was overwhelming; the tedious work, coupled with the heat and humidity as we tried to make our way through a tangled bean field, was nothing short of misery. I hated every minute of it.

Of course, there were some jobs that were essential to our operation, one of which was irrigating the crops. My sisters and I became quite proficient at loading the pipe trailer with thirty-foot aluminum irrigation pipe, which we then laid out at the ends of the fields, sometimes a quarter mile long – a muscle-building task that always left us dirty, sweaty messes. It also wasn't unusual to find a skunk hiding in the pipes. The creatures enjoyed hiding out in there, and it could be a challenge to lure them out so we wouldn't get sprayed. We could easily spend an entire morning during the growing season hauling pipe from one field to another. We did the job without complaining; in fact, opening the gates on the pipe so the water could run down the row was one of my favorite tasks and we had to switch the rows twice a day. Many times, it was necessary to dig a channel to make sure the water flowed down the right row.

Riding in the back of the pickup was our mode of transportation for many years, and each time I climbed in it I felt like I was being sentenced to death. There were no straps or seatbelts to secure me, no handles or anything else to hold onto. My sisters and I would grab the side of the box, every muscle tensed and our hair flying wildly as Dad flew down the gravel road. Suddenly he would slam on the brakes, sending the pickup skidding across the gravel, then he would throw it in reverse and turn around in the middle of the road. The worst was when he backed halfway down into the ditch, not out of necessity but for the irresistible thrill of scaring the life right out of me. Every. Damned. Time.

With our father, it was always a guessing game. We never knew what he would think of next, only that it would probably be scary, maybe even terrifying. One time he drove along the forty-foot sidewall of a water reuse pit (no place for a pickup to drive, especially with precious cargo in the back). It was extremely steep, and I remember climbing to the high side of the truck so I wouldn't fall out. For sure I left my body that day and lost even more trust, already in such short supply, for my dad. *He sure can be an ass,* I would secretly tell myself on such occasions; but as always, I felt powerless to change a thing or say a word.

I might have thought this was normal farm life, except none of my friends who lived on farms were ever put into these situations. That said, we were a source of mirth for some of our neighbors, also farmers, who would stop by. I remember more than one occasion when they watched us perform some ridiculous job, their bellies shaking with laughter, that Dad had commanded us to do. This made me more distrustful of males as sources of protection or comfort, and even more determined not to let my father's behavior get the best of me. I'd probably never heard the saying, "What doesn't kill you makes you stronger" at that age, but I was certainly living it!

There was no time for idle play in our family, and the idea of taking time to "just be" was simply unheard of. Any stolen moments were abruptly interrupted by calls of "Dad's home!" that would send us running to our rooms like birds scattering from telephone wires. I'll never forget the "deer in the headlights" look on Terri's face one particular day when the call of his arrival went out. She had been engaged in the unpardonable sin of sitting on the couch reading a book. Other times, she would give him a "what the fuck" look – the only one of us with the courage to do so – before beating a hasty path to her room.

There was also this sense of responsibility that ran through our veins and into our bones. If there was work to be done, which there always was, we were on it instantly. I have no doubt we were born with it, though it was certainly reinforced on a daily basis by the harsh commands of our father. Either way you look at it, this sense of responsibility was rooted in, and supported by, the belief systems of many previous generations who were just trying to survive life on the farm. We had unconsciously kept up the practice, even though it was no longer necessary and did not serve our family's well-being. We also found ourselves thriving on the sense of being responsible mostly for other's sakes, rather than our own. If someone had a problem, "by Gawd" we would meddle and fix it no matter what the cost! The idea of letting go and trusting our Higher Power was not a thing in our family. It was "hold on for dear life," tighten the grip and then grit your teeth and tighten the grip some more.

If I had to describe our family dynamic in one word, it would be "enmeshed." In psychological terms, enmeshment is a collection of codependent behaviors that include a lack of boundaries; a lack of privacy; over-involvement with each other's relationships; and fear and guilt of not fulfilling our role in the family unit. There's often extreme loyalty, shared emotions, thoughts, feelings, and opinions. While our family appeared to be close, we were missing the deeper, honest connection of honoring each individual's uniqueness. Heidi and I felt a lot of confusion because of this lack of emotional closeness, especially to our dear, sweet mother.

For the most part, Mom was unaware of how my sisters and I were handling life. She spent nearly every minute of her day focused on keeping my father satisfied, and herself far from his next fit of rage. She was always toiling away at something, whether it was getting the next meal prepared and served, digging into the tough brome grass, trying to loosen it up for the beautiful flowers she wanted to plant and nourish, or one of her countless other tasks. This left her with no time or energy to spare for our emotional well-being. Looking back, I realize that she was simply trying to survive a relationship with an unpredictable man who might come home at any minute and create unnecessary chaos. Mom was always on alert!

Thank goodness we were blessed with Grandmother Harrington's presence once a month when she came to do the bookkeeping for the farm and spend time with us. After I had been waiting for what seemed like hours, I'd see her Buick coming up the driveway.

Heidi best described the occasion: "It was like Christmas when Grandmother arrived!"

"Hi, sweetheart," she'd say every time I met her at the end of the sidewalk, "It's so good to see you!"

"Hi, Grandmother!" I'd shout, jumping up and down before offering to carry her bag into the house.

Then she would take her big, soft-as-silk hands and embrace my cheeks and we'd look into each other's brown eyes. At that moment I knew I was loved completely by the most important person in my life, and it was all that mattered. Grandmother Harrington was my saving grace and my reason to be.

Recently I found a letter I wrote to her. It read: "Dear Grandmother, I love you very much and *I hope you love me also*. Love, Abbi."

I had my answer every time I saw her.

She was always a great protector of her four granddaughters and would squeal, "Tommy, stop that!" whenever Dad's roughhousing with us became too much for her. Grandmother's stays were absolutely delightful as she always made time to listen to us play the piano and made sure she connected with each of us in some way. I was always glad to see that she treated my mother with so much respect and love. She was well aware that her son wasn't easy to live with, and very grateful to Mom for being such a good wife to him.

We did have some pretty solid traditions during those growing-up years, the most enjoyable of which was the Sunday afternoon touch football games. All of us sisters played, along with Dad and usually one of Terri's boyfriends. It was the one moment in time when Dad was decent, despite his competitive nature he encouraged me as long as I was trying my best. He was always so proud when he passed the ball to one of us and a touchdown was scored.

The other Sunday tradition centered around the long, S-shaped table in our flagstone floor living room, where the extended family would gather for one of Mom's incredible meals. It always took her several hours to fix, especially since she wouldn't let anyone into the kitchen to help her, but the food was so delicious the agony of growling tummies was forgotten after the first bite.

Sadly, those family meals were also occasions, when I left my body. Dad would start political arguments with Mom's side of the family, and the dinner table would get so tense I couldn't handle it. I had no understanding of politics, but I felt so sad for my relatives who were being annihilated by my ruthless father, for no good reason. I had been taught to be kind to people, especially when they were guests in our home. But one of Dad's favorite pastimes was arguing, making himself right and the other person wrong. He met his match with a few family members who appeared to enjoy the bantering, while others simply refused to engage with him. I remember sitting at the table daydreaming and waiting for the moment when I could be excused. When I think about it, I wonder why those folks kept coming back, Sunday after Sunday, year after year? As my mother often said, "They were a glutton for punishment!" I sometimes wonder if that described how my sweet, precious momma may have felt at times.

CHAPTER 4

Circle Your Wagons

Circle Your Wagons [idiomatic]. To prepare to defend against an attack or criticism.

~Wiktionary

I first learned the phrase "circle your wagons" from the same woman who taught me about unconditional love: my beloved grandmother. Eunice Helen (Kniss) Harrington was born to Peter and Kate (Ulmer) Kniss in Sutton, Nebraska in 1905, and along with her brother Kuni, grew up on the family farm. Sutton was a German-Russian community, and our family delighted in the dumplings filled with cottage cheese and a custard pie known as kuchen, that Grandmother often shared with us. Her signature dish while I was growing up was Yorkshire Pudding and my sisters and I still delight in serving it at holiday gatherings.

After graduating from Sutton High School in 1923, she attended York College for a time and took some accounting classes through a home study program, all while teaching school in the Lushton area.

Grandmother Eunice was elegant and stately, gentle and passionate; she was also highly intelligent and never stopped learning about the world she was a part of. She adorned herself with large pearl earrings and a matching pearl necklace, and the most stunningly beautiful solitaire diamond that had belonged to my grandfather. After he passed away, she had it reset and wore it for the rest of her days.

She also lived in a lovely sprawling brick ranch house, located in the Arbor Heights neighborhood of York, that she and Grandfather built in the 1950s. It was always a treat when my sisters and I got to spend the night at her house. It was a lot for her to care for all three of us, but Grandmother managed superbly. She used to make refrigerator biscuits and serve them to us while we were watching television in the den. I remember peeling each layer of biscuit off and letting it melt in my mouth, just like I allowed the love I felt from her to slowly melt my heart. I loved taking a bath in her feminine, luxurious bathroom with the white fluffy rugs and a wall heater that kept me warm. It was always a competition to see who got to sleep in the bay window in her bedroom. I loved to look out of that magical window and up at the stars, somehow knowing that I belonged to the expansive Universe. I felt so loved in those moments.

Some of the most memorable times with our grandmother were when she and her neighbor took us to the Ace Drive-Inn, in York. Each table had a mini jukebox, and we had a blast choosing music from the '60s and playing it while we waited for baskets of the fried chicken in all its greasy splendor.

Another favorite was the well-known local eatery Chances "R." Of the many times we dined there, one occasion stands out. While waiting for our food my sisters and I were arguing back and forth as sisters often do, when suddenly Grandmother slammed her hand down on the table and barked, "Dammit, girls, I said stop it!"

We were shocked. Grandmother Eunice seldom lost her temper with us and I'm certain I had never heard her swear before. Terri, Heidi and I exchanged sheepish looks which included a couple of mumbled giggles, but what I remember most is slithering back in the booth, hoping to disappear. She got our attention, that is for sure and I am certain we ate in peace and were on our best behavior after that experience.

It wasn't long after that incident that Grandmother taught us to "circle our wagons" when we felt bullied by each other, or anyone else for that matter. We wouldn't dare fight at the dinner table at home – Dad surely would have poked us with a fork – but we eagerly soaked up this sage advice from our beloved Grandmother. "Circle your wagons" became her go-to whenever we were going at it.

"The pioneers would shout out 'Circle your wagons!'" she explained, "whenever they were being attacked. It meant for them to form a barrier the enemy couldn't cross." It is interesting that, as noted above, the dictionary defines "circling your wagons" as "preparing for attack or criticism." My grandmother was well aware of her beloved son's biting criticism of himself and others, and I've often wondered whether she was also teaching us to prepare ourselves for his attacks.

For all her strength, even she was not immune to them. It broke my heart when Dad made fun of her, sometimes bringing her to tears. I only witnessed that a few times, thank goodness. Truthfully, he cherished the ground his mother walked on, but every now and then he would get the best of her, as he did with most people who knew him. He also clearly sought her approval. When she came to the farm during the growing season, he would take her for a ride to see all the fields and show her how nice the crops looked. I remember wishing I could go along but I never asked; I understood it was their sacred time together.

Regardless of her rationale, whenever I heard the phrase "circle your wagons" I knew I needed to improve my behavior to honor the grandmother I adored. Today I feel the phrase signifies a way for the women in our family to feel empowered, to stand strong and courageous together, in the face of life's challenges.

Grandmother rarely asked anything of us, so when she did we happily obliged. We were to call her "Grandmother" instead of "Grandma," as she felt it commanded more respect. She also taught us to answer the telephone at home with a formal greeting, such as "Harrington residence, Abbi speaking." I can still remember the three of us rushing toward the ringing phone, and how confident and businesslike I felt when I beat my sisters to it and raised the phone to my ear to speak. It was one of the first ways in which I began using my voice.

It is impossible to convey all the ways in which my grandmother influenced the woman I am today. She certainly taught me the importance of always striving to keep learning and lending a helping hand. After Grandfather passed, she became very involved with the United Methodist Church and eventually became the National President of United Methodist Women. In that role she traveled the world visiting UMW mission projects, mostly orphanages in small, poverty-stricken countries. She was passionate when it came to equal rights for women and spoke of a woman's worth at every opportunity.

In one of her numerous speeches she declared, "One of America's greatest natural resources is woman power, but it is not being properly used. The manpower and brainpower of our nation could be enormously increased, our capacity for growth greatly enlarged and the future brighter and more secure if this power would be used effectively."

She also passionately encouraged women to, "Be more than money-raisers and interpreters. We are more, we need spiritual growth, education, and leadership training."

Were someone to ask me about my Grandmother's philosophy on life, I would have to borrow the following words from an unknown author: "If you are more fortunate than others, it's better to build a longer table than a taller fence." Certainly, Grandmother had a great degree of compassion and love for all human beings. She truly never placed herself above anyone and embraced all of mankind in a very loving manner. She just couldn't give enough.

In 1954, my grandparents sponsored a Latvian family through the Methodist Church. Like many Latvians, Anna Purins and her daughter Ausma Buda had endured hardships that were unimaginable to most White Americans at the time. Their tiny country had been invaded, first by the Russians in 1940, then the Nazis the following year, only to be returned to Soviet control toward the end of World War II. Ausma's husband, who had joined the Latvian army, promised he would join her and their baby, Aiji, later. Heartbroken to leave her husband and homeland behind, Ausma eventually fled with her mother and daughter to Germany, where they found themselves living in a misplaced persons' camp. Her husband ended up staying in Lativa after the war and married another woman.

After much bureaucratic red tape, Anna, Ausma and Aija finally arrived at Ellis Island and traveled by train to Nebraska. My grandparents helped them set up a home in York, and Ausma worked as a nurse at a medical clinic for more than three decades. Over the years our families became one, and though Ausma went through many tough times she always found a way to make it through, usually with a big smile. She had a huge support system and was dearly loved by many people. In the fall of 2020, she passed away at age ninety-seven after contracting the Covid-19 virus. She is sorely missed and will always be a hero in my book.

Grandmother also abhorred racial bias, and in the 1960's she showed her support for the Civil Rights Movement. I remember distinctly the time she walked out of her adult Sunday school class at the First United Methodist Church in York with an uncharacteristic look of anger on her face.

"That man is such a bigot!" she said in her quiet, ladylike voice, but her feelings were clear.

Whoever the man was, my guess is she handed it right back to him when he spoke from a perspective of White superiority and his unfounded fear of those different from himself. Let's hope she planted a seed.

In the early '70s she moved to Omaha to make travel, which she did often as the national president of the UMW, more convenient. When we spent time with her in the summers, she would take us out on the town to show us the strides the Black community had made to rise out of poverty and suppression. We toured the first Black radio station, which she'd had a hand in starting. It was an accomplishment of which she was immensely proud.

Our favorite place to visit was Peony Park, and though she took us there often she made sure to let us know that it too had been touched by bigotry. "Blacks are not allowed to swim in the pool," she lamented sadly, "because some people think they are dirty."

Hearing those words made me feel both disgusted and confused. I hoped she never took us there again! Eunice Harrington was so full of love and compassion for those who were oppressed, it was unthinkable for her to see a brother or sister in pain and not attempt to lift them up. Aside from her family, helping others was her purpose for being.

Even when we weren't together, Grandmother always managed to let us know that we were in her thoughts. If the weather turned stormy, we all knew it was just a matter of time before she called.

"Hello, Abbi?" she'd say with worry in her voice "This is Grandmother. Is everyone home safe and sound?" I would always reassure her we were all doing fine and that another storm had left us unscathed.

She was my everything and I deeply cherish my memories of her. There is no doubt that my grandmother's energy or spirit is still by my side, encouraging me to keep learning, growing, and standing up for those less fortunate. Her spirit keeps me safe, comforted, and loved, just as she did in life.

One of the most fitting honors bestowed upon Grandmother was that of *Honorary Degree of Doctor of Humane Letters,* at Nebraska Wesleyan University. The decree follows:

> *For the concern for the status of women in a society which needs desperately the wise counsel of all thinking creatures, for positive leadership exerted for the correction of evils in all facets of life; for the courage to express convictions in a clear and forceful manner, without concern for what others might say or think; for willingness to share of those assets with which God has provided you, to the betterment of all mankind; for the patience with which you deal with those whom you disagree, as you seek, with neither malice nor with force, to extend the influence of your own beliefs; and for your complete allegiance to a code of values to which all of humankind should aspire.*

EUNICE KNISS HARRINGTON, it is my privilege because of the authority invested in me as the president of Nebraska Wesleyan University, and upon the recommendation of the faculty and the Board of Trustees of this institution of higher education, to hail you now as a person worthy of this distinction, and to confer upon you the Honorary degree of Doctor of Humane Letters.

Vance D. Rogers, President
Nebraska Wesleyan University
June 5, 1961

CHAPTER 5

What is a Normal Family Anyway?

"Family ties mean that no matter how much you might want to run from your family, you can't."

~Author unknown

Dad spent the late 1960s and '70s expanding the farming operation. He also decided it was time to build a house. I'm not talking about your normal two-story, wood-frame house that most farm families would build, but one designed by an architect from Colorado whose specialty was designing ski lodges!

It was a great home – made of cement block with slanted bookshelves in the den, orange carpet on the walls, light switches underneath the carpet, and a humongous living room with a flagstone floor and a mammoth fireplace in the center. There was even a swinging couch attached with log chains to a ceiling beam. I would have enjoyed it much more if my schoolmates hadn't started saying, "The Harringtons are rich, the Harringtons are rich," with increasing regularity. It made me feel as though we were different, that we didn't belong.

I remember on several occasions thinking to myself, *"Why can't we just have a normal house like everyone else around here?"* Of course, I never would have said such thing out loud in front of my father. The teasing continued until the end of high school, though I eventually became numb to it and moved on.

Most winters our family would take a week off school and farm work and head to Colorado to ski the Rocky Mountains. Of course, Dad was not concerned with teaching his daughters to ski and would go hit the slopes on his own. Mom was the one who helped us get started and then we taught ourselves. I knew in my dad's eyes "only the strong survive" though it would be many years before I understood what he was trying to accomplish by leaving us to our own devices on the ski slopes, or in the cornfields. My sisters and I made the best of it and enjoyed the time staying in a condominium.

My dad was an activist at heart and had a deep concern for our underground water supply. In the 1970s he begged the local NRD (Natural Resources District) to monitor how much water farmers were using to irrigate, as we were in the midst of a several-year drought, and he felt farmers were wasting water when irrigating their crops. He always did his research when developing his ideas, and many mornings we found him sitting at the breakfast table writing out the talking points he planned to deliver to boards, whether it be the NRD or the York County Commissioners. He also routinely wrote letters to the editor of the local newspaper, and the editor, who was quite conservative, always enjoyed debating back and forth about the ideas Dad presented. My dad, who took the "Freedom of Speech" amendment very seriously, was always happy to oblige.

My father had a strong desire for his daughters to get a decent, well-rounded education. He felt a fair amount of disdain for the small, rural, public school we attended. He sensed the conservative nature of the school leaders and on more than one occasion showed up at a school board meeting, trying to convince them to consolidate with other small schools in the area. His thought was that with more students the school could offer a more diversified curriculum and more opportunities. His idea was met with the utmost resistance by all board members. Dad was a man before his time; he knew what he was talking about, but no one was ready to hear it. (Indeed, it would take nearly forty years before schools finally started consolidating. By then they were forced to, as the rural areas had become less populated and didn't have enough funding to keep the schools open.) When I was in the sixth grade my dad went to the school board to request that girls be allowed to wear pants on the cold winter days, especially because we waited outside for the bus to pick us up. He did get them to agree with that. Whew! We've come a long way, baby!

Dad was also instrumental in getting a girls' basketball program started at our high school. He was aware of the rules of Title 9 and felt that girls deserved to have a winter sport to play, just as the boys did. He won, and my sisters and I participated and played on the team. That first year was pretty hilarious, as very few of us had ever bounced a basketball, let alone shot one into the hoop! We had a brave teacher who volunteered to be our coach, and I'm sure he needed a few beers after the games.

Ours was one of the first small schools to offer the sport to girls, which meant our first game was against a much larger school with some truly superb athletes. I can imagine that after watching us for a while Dad began to wonder what the heck he had been thinking when he undertook this particular cause. Being the dutiful daughter I was, I worked on my basketball skills during the summer and Dad even put up a basketball goal in the machine shed for me so I could practice and, hopefully, improve.

My father was very easily bored, and he was always searching for something new and different to investigate, sometimes to the dismay of my mother, my sisters, and me. When I was in junior high, he decided to quit farming, have a farm sale, and move to the Australian outback. Of course, I was horrified at the idea, and mortified when my new nickname at school became "Skippy," referring to Skippy the Kangaroo. Thankfully, after Dad and Mom spent time in Australia, he decided to stay stateside.

As the farm kept growing and changing Dad decided to expand his livestock to include hogs as well as cattle. He always kept abreast of the latest and greatest investments, and he incorporated those ideas into the several hog confinement buildings he built. This new venture meant there was once again plenty of work for us girls to do. He built a farrow to finish hog operation, which meant that the sows gave birth to their litter of piglets in the farrowing house and then we fed them until they were "finished" and ready for slaughter – usually about six months. The sows had, on average, two-and-one-half litters a year and raised eight or nine piglets each time. When we weren't in school my sisters and I were in charge of operating the hog business. No longer did the Harrington girls have ridiculous, random jobs to perform – we were now pig farmers!

All through high school, we had pig chores each morning before school and at night after sports practice. On weekends we spent most of our time working with the pigs. Figuring out when a particular sow was going to farrow was one of our bigger challenges, and there were many mornings when the first person to arrive at the farm found that the blessed event had already occurred.

"Get over here now," they'd say when they called over to the house, "There's a litter of baby pigs running around the sow lot!"

The rest of us would hightail it over there, in the crisis mode we had been taught so well by our father. We would then hop in the tractor, load up the momma and the baby pigs, and haul them into their crate in the farrowing barn where they would raise their piglets for the next thirty days. Since they would be raised in confinement the piglets would need their needle teeth clipped and their tails docked; the males would be castrated and the runts, more than likely, knocked in the head. The three of us became proficient in all these tasks, without so much as a nudge from our father. We knew what the recourse would be if we neglected any of these duties, so we just obeyed and did as we were told.

Dad decided to bring a little culture to our family and enrolled in the Japanese Trainee Program through the National 4-H Council, which brought college-age men from Japan to our farm to learn about raising pigs and to improve their English. The "Japanese boys," as we called them, would invite us over for a genuine Japanese dinner and share gifts from their culture with us. They taught us how to count to ten in Japanese and always had their translation dictionary handy when we communicated. It was a bright spot in our youth and our first experience with a culture other than the Euro-German community we were immersed in, living in the Midwest.

Along with pig farming, my sisters and I were trained to drive the tractor to cultivate the corn and soybeans. Terri was the first one to experience the long, hot, and sweaty dusty days on a tractor without a cab, and, true to form, she made it work for her. She would wear her bikini underneath her work clothes, which she promptly removed after Dad dropped her off at the field, then up and down the rows of corn she went for hours on end. The tops of her legs became like burnt toast, but she loved the tan.

Heidi and I would trade off running the cultivator after chores were done, and many times when she came to take my place she'd say rather snottily, "Abbi, you are off your row!"

"No, I'm not you crab apple!" I'd retort, then mumble a few choice words to myself as I hopped off the tractor. *Man, she's a bitch, what's up with her?*

Ah, sisterly love. Heidi and I were best of friends in our younger years but by the time we were teenagers an unspoken competition had developed between us. Heidi was a natural farmer and mechanic and loved working with the cows, while the farm jobs just didn't feel natural to me. She was also quite popular with the boys and dated quite often, while I experienced none of that. It seemed on both fronts I was always trying to keep up with her and found myself falling short.

Every now and then we got a reminder just how dangerous farming can be. One day, as Terri was driving the neighbor's tractor along the side of the road to spray weeds in the ditch, a tire went over the edge. The tractor rolled into the ditch, and thankfully Terri instinctively knew to jump in the opposite direction and escaped uninjured. *Archangel Michael, was that you?*

One can just imagine Dad's panic when he drove up and saw the tractor on its side, knowing his daughter was driving it! He jumped out of the pickup, ran over to Terri and started patting her down.

"Are you okay, are you sure you are okay?"

Terri, a bit stunned and amazed that she survived said, "Yeah, I'm okay, and I'm really sorry, Dad." She felt bad because the tractor belonged to our neighbor, but today what still stands out in her mind are those precious ten minutes Dad was able to show compassion toward her.

Thanks to Terri, that same neighbor's other tractor met a similar demise. She brought it to a stop on the hillside by our underground silo but unbeknownst to her, didn't quite get the tractor into the park position. Later, when I went to hop on the tractor to move some pigs, it wasn't where she'd said she left it. I called her.

"Terri, where's the tractor?

Impatiently she replied, "On the driveway right by the silo."

Except it wasn't. She insisted, so I went to look again, this time daring to look in the silo itself. Sure enough, there was the tractor, its backend sticking up in the air. Once again, we had to call a tow truck for assistance.

My sisters and I weren't the only ones who needed rescuing from time to time. One cloudy day, Dad was working in a reuse pit with his D8 caterpillar, a medium-sized bulldozer. The reuse pit was designed to catch rainwater for irrigation purposes. The bulldozer got stuck in the mud and then it began to rain. I'll never forget the panic I felt as I stood by and watched the water rise alongside the bulldozer while Dad frantically kept trying to work the machine out of the mud, to no avail. The tow truck finally arrived and was able to pull the bulldozer safely up out of the pit. Though we always somehow managed to escape serious physical harm, panic had its way with me every time.

We also had a couple of big fires on our farm, which were both traumatizing and terrifying. Some of our outbuildings had faulty wiring and Dad was known for not keeping things well maintained. I don't know what started the blaze in the hog confinement building, but it burned to the ground along with quite a few sows and litters, and grower pigs. Oh, how my heart broke as we put the carcasses on the skid loader to be hauled away. The only thing I wasn't going to miss inside that hog building were the rats that I'd see every time I turned on the lights to do chores. I'd always remember the horror story Dad shared about having a rat crawl up his jeans when he was helping shell corn. Of course, he told how he squeezed the rat's head and killed it.

Then there were the causes that lit a fire under our activist father, and he never hesitated to pull us girls into his storm. One summer we were deep in a drought, and after weeks without rain our neighbor's dryland milo field was literally drying up. Dad felt bad and decided to haul irrigation pipe over there, but to do it he would need his gang of three. The next thing we knew my sisters and I were helping him lay pipe all across the neighbor's field. Dad then proceeded to hand-dig a trench across the county road and placed irrigation pipe in the trench to get the water where it needed to go. He even put up a homemade "Road Closed" sign! As you can imagine the county sheriff was out there in no time, ordering him to remove the pipe that was blocking the road. Undeterred, Dad called the television station and told them what was going on. A camera crew came out from Lincoln and captured my sister laying in the trench while the county employee sat in the road grader, ready to fill it in at the sheriff's order. Eventually, the sheriff won and there was no more watering the neighbor's milo. They could have arrested Dad and hauled his ass to jail, but they probably knew he would fight them all the way and figured it wasn't worth it. I also believe they knew he had a good heart and didn't mean to cause any harm.

Another one of Dad's projects was fighting the ever-increasing land taxes being imposed on farm ground. He refused to pay these taxes and for a time held them in escrow. His goal was to incite a revolt but despite his valiant efforts only a few neighbors followed along. I remember having to read a letter protesting the tax increases to a meeting of the county commissioners because my dad was out of town. Looking back, I am shocked that I was so willing, but how could I refuse when Dad had placed such faith in me? At that time, it was important for me to support his causes, and that helped me overcome, at least temporarily, my considerable shyness. As for the land taxes, they continued to rise and are still an unresolved issue some forty years later!

Eventually, Dad lost interest in drumming up involvement for his latest cause. He realized his circle of business friends were never going to join his crusade to improve the lot for farmers. They were never going to fight for lower taxes on farmland or try to prevent the state from taking a farmer's land to make bigger ditches or wider highways. So, while he certainly continued to enjoy antagonizing his more conservative peers, he shifted his considerable energies to his other great love: sports.

Dad started playing the game of squash quite regularly. He even convinced the city of York to put in a squash court at the new community center. There was very little competition for him in York, so he started playing in Lincoln, Omaha, and eventually Denver, Colorado. He would go on to win tournaments all over the U.S. and Canada. There was nothing he loved more than a challenge, competition, and a good, old-fashioned fight.

During my high school years Mom and Dad would often head out to a squash tournament in some other state, leaving us four girls at home, large and in charge for the entire weekend. To me and my sisters, those times were sacred and highly anticipated. All disputes were put aside, we had a blast cooking, making sure all the pig chores were done before playing the game of PIT – a trading game where you bid on commodities like corn, oats, beans and wheat. The goal was to end up with the bull card, NOT the bear card, and we spent hours at the long S-shaped table, shouting and laughing at whoever was left holding the bear. Those weekends were among the very few times when the four of us were able to cut loose and simply enjoy each other's company without the many stresses we otherwise carried with us when Dad was commander-in-chief.

CHAPTER 6

Lost in The Shuffle

"Not until we are lost do we begin to understand ourselves."

~Henry David Thoreau

When it came time for me to leave home for college, I wasn't prepared, mentally or emotionally. My mess of a childhood had left me feeling lost, empty and alone, with no idea who I was or what I was doing. I was still clinging to my mom and dad, but they were in the "done parenting" mode. "You have to go to college," they told me, "You can't stay here." I was so homesick during my freshman year of college, I fell into a very dark place and failed to complete my classes for three semesters in a row.

The support I received from my mother could be summed up in one matter-of-fact statement. "You need counseling. I can't help you."

I took her advice and, over the course of my adult life, saw more than a handful of different counselors. I finally came to the realization that when you are pressed down during your childhood by an overbearing father, and your mother is basically in the same position as you, and thus unable to help, depression often results. In my case, the depression was nothing more than a disconnect from my true self, the result of the demeaning manner in which my father treated me in my formative years.

Recently, when I was having somewhat of an off day and I was sitting and staring out the window because that's all I wanted to do, I suddenly heard my father's voice: "That son of a bitch isn't worth anything."

To think that voice still shows up, astounds me! I certainly took it on and owned it up until now. In my family, a person only had worth if they were physically working at least eight hours a day. There was no value found in sitting around or just hanging out. I can't begin to tell you what that does to one's nervous system.

Ironically, it was my father who gave me the permission to finally take control and start pulling myself up by my bra straps. After a horrible attempt at college, I told him I was coming back to the farm to raise pigs, and he agreed. As for what my mother said about having to go to college, I no longer cared. I'm pretty certain Mom was only looking out for my best interests – she very much regretted not finishing college before getting married and moving to the farm and she didn't want her girls to suffer a similar fate. However, I knew what I needed was the familiarity of the work and the comfort of home.

During this time Dad was living part-time in Denver, as he went there for squash competitions, and my sister Terri was attending law school there.

Shortly after my return to the farm, I became acquainted with a local pig farmer, fell in love, and married at age twenty. By the time I was twenty-two we were parents of two precious boys, Kyle and Casey, and I gave up my hog business to be a stay-at-home mom. But though life was good, and the boys were very easy to care for, I was a mess emotionally. It seemed like the trauma I suffered growing up was coming back to haunt me. Once again, I found myself feeling lonely and isolated with no one to connect with. I reached out to my mom but by that time she had followed Dad to Denver and wasn't available to support me. We did write some letters back and forth and she suggested she was willing to strengthen our mother-daughter bond, but when it came time to walk the talk, there was nothing there. She had her own trauma from being married to my father and apparently felt pretty empty, with nothing left to give.

Feeling desperate and unfulfilled, I walked through the doors of divorce when my sons were only two and four years old. I was in a place where I needed to find myself, and at that time being married was not conducive to my journey. It was as difficult as it was freeing though. I had to find my strength and make very tough decisions that I knew were in my best interests but were terrifying all the same. Shortly after the divorce I returned to the university and earned a I received a degree in education all while single parenting. For many years to come I was torn apart by the guilt and shame of our marriage ending.

Perhaps even more earth-shaking was my parents' divorce. No one was more shocked than my father, who couldn't believe that after twenty-five years my mother was walking away from him and the control he wielded over her. This was an extremely difficult time for him, and he was even suicidal for a time. It was Terri, then a public defender in Denver, who helped him work through the darkest days of his life.

As for my mother, she finally found her wings. She enrolled in school, earned a degree in psychology, and went on to work full-time until she was well into her seventies. It was oddly similar to the path I had taken, with one exception: my mother, it seemed, never really wanted to look at the trauma she had endured during their marriage, whereas I knew that in order to become who I truly was I would have to meet my stuff head-on.

It was inspiring for me to see my mother take back her power and develop a life just for her. I believe that when she married my father at nineteen, she was not running toward him so much as running from her own family. While she enjoyed motherhood and her four daughters, she just couldn't catch a break from my father and his emotional immaturity. It was painful as a young girl to watch her cry over the kitchen sink (which happened quite often) because of some hurtful comment he had made to her. I also noticed that Mom very rarely stopped working, unless it was to sleep.

What I don't remember is her ever standing up to him and saying, "No, Tom! It's not okay for you to mistreat me!" She just kept taking it and smiling until she could no longer control the tears.

Mom didn't bring us girls into the disharmony she was experiencing, though she did lean on Terri sometimes. Bless her heart, she was like an energizer bunny, she just kept going and going and going.

Luckily for Dad, soon after the divorce he found a wonderful woman to love him in a way that helped him feel more worthy. They were married and life was good until he had a bike accident at a busy intersection in downtown Denver. The front wheel of his bicycle disconnected from the the bike, he wasn't wearing a helmet, and he hit his head on the curb with great impact. He was hospitalized for several days with a severe concussion but rebounded quite well. Then, a few years later he was diagnosed with Parkinson's Disease, specifically, progressive supranuclear palsy, and life became very rough for him. All the athletic activities that had defined him and he had so enjoyed came to an abrupt end as moving his body became more and more difficult. Eventually, his muscles atrophied, he could no longer speak or feed himself, and he required twenty-four-hour care. As one could imagine, his mental health also deteriorated, and he had some pretty intense bouts with anger which was part of his grieving the loss of control he had fought for all his life. After almost five years of fighting the disease, he finally passed away peacefully from pneumonia at sixty years young.

At the time of his death, I was somewhat estranged from my father. Throughout my adult life I had waffled back and forth between trying to tolerate his childish behaviors and backing away when the anguish became too much. The final breaking point came when he got sick and threw fits of rage and anger because of what the disease was doing to him. At the time I was raising my boys alone and teaching school, and I simply didn't have the emotional or mental wherewithal to deal with his abuse.

Though I truly loved my father, after his death I began to feel more freedom in my life. I had learned very early to withdraw so as not to incur his wrath, and now it was as if a heavy weight had been lifted and I was finally free to explore who the hell I was, without criticism. At the same time, I was grateful for his presence in my life and the lessons he had imparted. He had been shackled by his emotional pain and I made a firm intention that I wasn't going to choose the same kind of life. I was beginning to get a sense of what it would be like to take back my authentic self, and I was excited!

Within two years of my father's passing, I was introduced to Kurt Kleinschmidt, a true man of the land. By that time, I had a teaching career I enjoyed, and Kyle and Casey were growing up and doing well. I had also put in ten years of intense but necessary work on my emotional health and was finally ready to share my life with someone. Kurt could be a man of few words, but he was stable, steady, and strong – a true salt-of-the-earth kind of guy and just what my heart and soul desired. When we met, he had been a bachelor for twenty years and was also ready for a lasting relationship. And boy, did he get it! He not only took on the role of husband but stepfather to Kyle and Casey, then ages nine and eleven. I continued teaching at the local elementary school until Kurt and I became parents to our son, Colton Kleinschmidt. Four years later we adopted our son, Cameron Kleinschmidt. A houseful of males, with not even a single female family pet! But hey, I'm satisfied being the Queen Bee. Over the years I've tried to scare Kurt off a few times, but he hasn't budged yet, and we just celebrated our twenty-fifth wedding anniversary!

CHAPTER 7

Not Your Ordinary Father

"I cannot think of any need in childhood as strong as the need for a father's protection."

~Sigmund Freud

I remember the first time I watched Mr. Rogers on television. I had no idea that a man could have a kind and gentle spirit such as he embodied. It quickly became my favorite show to watch and each time I did so with a sense of awe. It certainly gave me hope that not all men I encountered in my life would be as untrustworthy and unpredictable as my father. As an adult, whenever I encounter a gentleman, I relish the time I get to spend in their presence. President Barack Obama is a man I will always hold the highest regard and respect for. He has a heart of love for all people and did his very best to make our country a fair and equitable place for all humans.

As I look back on some letters I wrote to my dad as a young adult, I am pleasantly surprised, and a bit amused, by how much resolution I'd found since my childhood days. In one letter I would be loving on him and praising him, and in the next I was telling him I wished he would die! This indicated enormous growth, as even attempting to express an ounce of anger was sure to unleash a torrent of rage from him. After suppressing my feelings for so long, in my twenties I finally started to "unthaw" and allowed them to rise to the top. Since then, it has been a slow but steady journey back to the real me. I no longer hold him accountable for any of my struggles in life, for I know it has all been designed as my life lessons.

The following are two examples of these contradictory letters. The first was written in July of 1979, when I expressed love for him after he supported me through my decision to have an abortion. In the second letter, written in July of 1988, it is quite evident that I had become well-versed in expressing my anger!

Dearest Dad,

You have just been super to me lately and I really appreciate it. You have always been an important influence on me and the decisions that I choose to make. I have made many mistakes in my life already, but you have helped me to overlook them and go on, remembering that each mistake builds our character – if only a little bit.

I'll never know what I would have done without you this past couple of weeks, without your much-needed support. Listening to some of the girls talk today at the abortion clinic I realized they didn't even have the opportunity to share the burden with their fathers. It made me realize just how special our relationship is to one another.

Dad, you have done many things that I deeply respect you for. Some things are your hard work on this farm, your determination to make it right and make it work, your strong character, your willingness to accept and go on, your ability to pull things together, and last but not least is that never-ending spirit of trying to keep making things better –especially for your family.

My love for you will never die, it just keeps growing and growing and growing –stronger each day!

I love you!!
Abbi

Dear Dad,

After seeing you behave as you did over the fourth of July and the two weeks before that, I'm convinced you are a bastard! You don't deserve to live on this earth. I wish you would stop and listen for God because I know He would save you and listen to all your troubles – that you have been carrying around for fifty years.

Dad, I've got some real bad hurts way deep down inside and they keep trying to surface but I won't let them because I'm afraid the pain will be too great. I've always listened to you word for word, but as I've become healthier and healthier, I don't believe a word of your fucking bullshit!! You have inflicted hurt in me so bad. I don't know if I'll ever get rid of it.

I remember when I was probably about four and you ordered me to get up from the table and turn up the radio. I said, "No!" and you yelled and said, "Get over there, right now, God damn it!" You physically picked me up and pushed me towards the radio. I happened to be chewing on a string of pearls and I swallowed them in my upset, but I never told anyone, I was too scared. *(Note: That may well have been the last time I defied his word for many years.)*

You were never much of a father to me. You didn't come to school to see me in my activities and you never came to church. At Christmas time you laid on the couch and moaned while the rest of us tried to enjoy opening our gifts. You hated gifts!

In high school, I was never good enough, even though I tried my very best. That is probably one of my biggest issues with you. I never remember any praise from you. I sure wasn't going to get anything from Mom because she was always so busy cleaning her fucking house. (I know, I'm maddest at her.) Dad, do you know what the words, "I love you" mean? I wish you would have said them more often. It sure would have given my self-concept a boost! Dad, did you even care that I was alive?

I remember when you were going through your divorce and you would call me and cry like a baby. Did you ever stop to think what that felt like to me? What was I supposed to do – the daughter who was never good enough? All of a sudden you were going to suck from me for awhile? I sure wish you would get some help with your unresolved issues! It's so unfair for you to carry them around and then dump them on your daughters.

I've been so perfect throughout my twenty-nine years and you never notice! I don't need you in my life except maybe to give me some of your money to help me and my boys while I try to make it through school as a single mom.

I've tried to stand up to you and you're a bastard. You tell me I've got a chip on my shoulder – well guess what, asshole – you're it! You are so sick, dad. I love you enough to wish you'd get help. What do you think about two of your daughters in counseling? Ever think much about that?

You've been the most unpredictable circumstance in my life. I never knew how you'd come home – steamy angry or calm and pessimistic. Your mood determined how our nights would go. You'd say one thing and then later deny that you said it. You abused Heidi so badly!! You know what, Dad, you don't deserve the four daughters you have.

No human being has to even step foot in the door around people like yourself. You are cruel, unfair, nasty, and controlling.

Your very pissed off daughter,
Abbi

Fifteen years later I was still processing. In another letter written after his death, I stated that I was still so angry and emotionally unstable and that I wasn't even sad he was gone. I wrote, "There just really wasn't a part of him I enjoyed. I could not trust how he would treat me or my family. Why do I still give him so much power in my life?" I went on to express that I hoped I could give my power to God instead.

My dad made it known that he didn't believe in God. I truly believed then that he felt he had all the power he ever needed inside of him. He absolutely loved to control and manipulate his daughters and wife. From the way he behaved, it was as if he thought he *was* God! I now know for sure that my Dad's fear loomed so large it took over and ran his life; he lived from the place of fear.

A "love-hate relationship" – that would be the best way for me to describe the connection I had with my father. There were times when I knew intuitively that he truly loved and cared for me, and then there were times when he was so self-absorbed that he couldn't see beyond the end of his nose. He was very quick to judge most of the time, although there were a few exceptions, and any confidence I thought I had could be wiped away in an instant by the words he spoke to me. I basically learned not to argue with him, and as an adult, keeping my distance from him was my best defense against the angst, he would inevitably project onto me. It has taken a lot of work for me to be able to say that I'm not only glad I survived my childhood, but grateful every day for the opportunities for growth that I continue to have because I was his daughter.

What follows is an article the Rocky Mountain News published about my father's love for the game of squash.

Ex-Husker'd Rather Play Squash than Grow It
By Scott Stocker

Thirty years on the farm were enough for Tom Harrington. Instead of growing squash, the former Nebraska farmer decided to seriously take up the game of the same name.

Harrington worked, cultivating and refining his game until he became both the reigning two-time U.S. National Masters Champion and the Canadian National Masters Champion.

And now Harrington, who makes his home in Denver, has set his sights on yet another title.

Along with an estimated 10,000 masters' athletes from around the world, the 52-year-old Harrington will head to Toronto, Canada in August to participate in The First Masters Games.

The concept is similar to the Olympics and officials hope the games will be held every four years. But then, they will be unlike the Olympics in several ways.

Only 22 sports (13 which are Olympic and only 3 team sports), will be contested by competitors from 69 countries from August 7-25. The focus of the games will be on individuals. There will be no national anthems nor national standings kept on medal winners, and it is hoped no politics or boycotts.

"Good Lord," said Harrington. "It sounds like a good thing to me. Canada seems to have a knack for this kind of thing and it certainly appears it will be handled in a first-class way." He continued, "It's hard to say at this time what the caliber of competition will be like. I have no idea what to expect, but I'll say this, I'll be disappointed if I don't win."

Harrington has been involved with squash for 15 years. Once he started to excel in the sport, he found it was hard to stay down on the farm.

"A friend of mine called me from Grand Island one day saying he found a game that would probably be of interest," said Harrington, who moved to Denver five years ago.

"We played and that particular afternoon I became absolutely addicted."

But there was a time when Harrington thought of giving up the game. "I played against Hashim Khan, who has since become a very dear friend, and he annihilated me. Losing is hard to swallow and it was frustrating. But Hashim (who has won every championship in the world in his career and whose name is synonymous with the game) kept me going."

It's been in the last three years that Harrington, who has been able to travel the world perfecting his game, started to roll. "Since squash is a tournament game (usually played from Friday to Sunday), the idea was to stay around to the finals. I just didn't like either going home or watching the others," he said. Right now, winning at squash is easier than growing it.

Thank God my dad had such great athletic ability that gave him something to be passionate about when farming became too frustrating and left him unsatisfied. Ultimately, I think that was his life plan – to find a way to be satisfied. Although I'm not sure he died a satisfied man, he sure gave it hell as long as he walked this earth. He also passed along his competitive edge to all his children and grandchildren, to that I can attest. Terri is a kick-ass mediation attorney who started her own law firm in Denver and has been a partner in the firm for forty years; Heidi, who graduated nursing school at age fifty, is very devoted to her career and has earned the Nurse of the Year Award. Jenni is the owner and operator of a nursery and garden center smack dab in the middle of rural Nebraska that continues to bloom and grow (pun intended). As for me, I spent years teaching some of the most wonderful children in the world; I am also the queen of devoting my life to learning, growing (and healing lots of old patterns, for myself as well as for past and future generations) and am soon to be a published author. Add to that the fact that we are all devoted to our own families and their families.

The following is a tribute to my father from his good friend, squash partner, and personal attorney, Richard Endicott, written in July 1994.

"He's Quite A Tom!"

"He's quite a Tom!" A curious response, but that's all they'd say when I'd ask folks from York County if they knew Tom Harrington. They couldn't describe him. Come to think of it, how do you describe a statue, a shadow, a rebel, the wind, a weed, velvet – or a stampede of cattle?

"He's quite a Tom." I've often pondered that response. What did it mean? The dictionary has some possible answers: "Really, truly, positively." Yes, those seem right on. And it says "Quite" means "a lot," "to a considerable degree." There was a lot of Tom Harrington. He was tall, athletic, and muscular. His Popeye forearms were those found on old-time dairymen, the ones who milked their own cows by hand. But I doubt if Tom ever stopped or stooped to milk a cow; he didn't like to sit for long. With his forearms like that no wonder he could hit a squash ball past me so easily. And his hands-- they were huge, rough, sandpaper vises. My hand – or a squash racket – disappeared in his hands. He gripped with the same determination and power that marked his competitive success and his life.

His personality was big too. As they say, "It was bigger than all outdoors." And that fit. Even the expanse of his farm was not enough for him. He needed a new country, new ventures, new challenges.

He could be loud and gruff, stubborn, sullen, irrational, domineering, and irreverent. He'd shout at his daughters with the tact of a bull whacker, argue with them like a lawyer, then sometimes get so quiet that they couldn't drag his words out with a calf puller. A barnyard iconoclast, he loudly ridiculed religion, government, and even Nebraska football. But to throw you off balance – like one of his off-speed squash shots – he'd occasionally hit you with softness and insight that would caress you with its sensitivity as it pulled you toward him.

He was as independent as his fence-hopping bulls and moody as a coddled cat. But selfish he was not. If you needed help, he was always willing to give it. He doggedly helped his neighbor get water to his drought-stricken field, even when he had to defy the sheriff to do it.

And he loved a good fight, especially if he knew he was right. He erected a sign when a belligerent neighbor's road dammed runoff water and backed it up in Tom's cornfield. The sign proclaimed for passersby: "Flood thy Neighbor!" That lawsuit went to the Nebraska Supreme Court. He lost. Next, he sued a spray pilot for stunting his beans with a weed killer. When he won less than he had hoped for, he turned to his lawyer – a veteran of many trials – and said, "Hope you have better luck in your second jury trial." He again went to court when the local elevator claimed his corn had wee-vils. "That's not my corn!" he thundered when the opposing lawyer poured a bag of corn onto a table and loosed a swarm of weevils in the courtroom. In that same case, he scolded the judge at a cocktail party for taking months to decide the case. "You're a judge, aren't you?" said Tom. "Then why don't you judge?" Somehow, he won that one.

A political gadfly, he pricked the conscience of the wasteful. In "Letters to the Editor" he waged campaigns to save the courthouse, save the trees, save the water. He was not only quick on the squash court but fast enough to stay ahead of the times. He was an innovator on the farm – a frontrunner in utilizing hog confinement houses, new corn varieties, homemade runoff pits, crossbred cattle, and center pivots. He caused quite a rumble among his York County neighbors when he accused them of overirrigating and depleting the water table. Once, when he stood up at a water meeting and advocated well monitoring years ago, his neighbors laughed and cursed him. Well, monitoring is now standard practice.

He was many things. Some bad, lots good. He was flawed, like all of us, but he was always a wondrous package of surprises. Best of all, he was my friend. That friendship was Tom himself – big, rough, unpredictable, unself-ish, honest, and enduring. I miss him.

The following article appeared in the Denver Athletic Club Newsletter when dad won the Athlete of the Year Award.

A MAN FOR ALL SQUASH COURTS AND MOST OCCASIONS

By Dennis Driscoll

It is not often that one is asked to write about a recently deceased dear friend, a superior competitor, one with an opinion on everything, a truly unique big-hearted wonderful, disrespectful slug like Tom. Ask Hashim, and I'm sure he will tell you, that the Denver Athletic Club and the local and national squash scene will never be the same.

Everyone who knew Tom will attest to the undeniable competitiveness, discipline, and work ethic he brought to every squash match, whether it was a pick-up game, or one for the national championship, which, by the way, he won on four different occasions. Those of us who knew him well enjoyed a frankness, a freshness, and a playfulness that energized every encounter, on and off the court. (Just ask Beth, his devoted beloved wife, and biggest fan.) Oh, how he could stir the pot!!

There will never be another like 'ole farm-bred Tom Harrington to pass by these parts. He leaves us with only fond, fun-filled memories; and I for one will truly miss that lovable, feisty, so-and-so.

Thomas W. Harrington

1933-1993

1984 National 50+ Hardball Champion

1985 National 50+ Hardball Champion

1985 National 50+ Softball Champion

1986 National 50+ Softball Champion

CHAPTER 8

An Honest Tribute to My Mother

"One of the most important relationships we'll have is the relationship with our mothers."

~Iyanla Vanzant

My mother, Karen Rauch Harrington, was born in Lincoln, Nebraska in 1936. She grew up in the city with her two hard-working parents and a brother who was two years younger than she. Her father, Russell Rauch, worked for the Lincoln Telephone and Telegraph Company for forty-two years. Her mother, Fern Helen Rauch, kept a very cozy house, was a great cook and enjoyed volunteering. She passed down a love of gardening and growing flowers that many family members are passionate about to this day.

Growing up, my sisters and I had many great times with our grandparents, usually involving a picnic in their backyard followed by a trip to Pioneer's Park in Lincoln where we'd climb up to the Indian statue. And I will always treasure the yummy Miller & Paine cinnamon rolls Grandmother warmed in her oven and served us for breakfast every time we stayed at her house.

As a young child I didn't always feel that sense of unconditional love from my mother that one expects from the woman who gave them life. Before I explain this, however, I must make it clear that it is not my intention to belittle my mother's character. She is one hell of a great woman and I adore her! Yet, I might not be writing this memoir had she not been my mom. You see, it was she who presented me some of my greatest learning opportunities (I call them gifts) in this lifetime. Mom taught me there is no love more important than the unconditional love I have for myself. She also taught me what it looks like to be a strong, independent woman and for that, I am so grateful.

That said, I also might not be writing this story if I had figured out these two gifts earlier in my life. I happened to be born with a highly sensitive capacity that my mother didn't understand, nor did she have the energy by the time her third daughter came along to try to figure anything out so she could be more present for my needs. The way I see it, my mother's energy was pretty well run dry by my father's neediness. This, coupled with the emotional detachment she likely inherited from her own mother, created our unique dynamic. I'm glad I had two older sisters who were very capable of caring for me when the adults in my life weren't up to it.

Mom used to go out and run a couple of miles down the gravel road from time to time, and I remember thinking, "Great! Here's my chance to get some attention – you know just Mom and Abbi time. I'll go join her!"

Of course, she went quite a bit faster than my short little legs could carry me, and before I knew it, she'd be down the road with me far behind.

"Mom," I'd cry out, "Wait for me!"

She'd turn around, still jogging, and say, "Catch up!" which I mistook for, "Catsup!"

I thought that was so funny – my mom running and yelling, "Catsup!" – and I'd get so distracted trying to figure out why she said it, that I'd lose sight of my mission and go back to the house.

That story perfectly exemplifies how I tried all my life to figure out how to have a closer relationship with my mom. It was the relationship that I needed and thought I had a birthright to, and though therapist after therapist tried to prop me up and teach me how to love myself and meet my own needs, I remained hell-bent on "solving the puzzle" so I could "feel" the love she had for me. How dammed exhausting! I can say that now.

I believe this is how I became an expert at people-pleasing. As I've mentioned, Mom never stopped working, and no matter how much she did, it seemed there was always something else to be washed, gardened, or put away. I decided if I did everything she asked of me and then some, she would somehow be able to connect with me. I'd clear the table, do the dishes, pick fruits and veggies from the garden, dust, and vacuum, and keep my room clean. While I am certain she was pleased with those things it didn't do anything to draw us closer.

I also watched her have a much more intimate relationship with my baby sister, Jenni, who came along four years after me. I developed jealousy toward my little sister and used to do whatever I could to antagonize her while we were growing up. Of course, I wasn't fully aware why I had ill will toward her, but looking back, it is now clear as a bell. It didn't help that when Jenni was born, I was continually told I couldn't hold her because I was too little, while Terri and Heidi got to hold her as much as they wanted, or so it seemed.

Becoming Mom's number one worker bee was only one of the ways I tried to get close to her. She used to spend hours in the kitchen cooking, and I would go in there and start running at the mouth about anything and everything. This became my go-to strategy, and one I engaged in quite often during my formative years. Though I never had the undivided attention I so desperately longed for, at least I was in her physical presence.

By the time I became a mother, with Mom living five hundred miles away, she spent years "wishing" she lived nearby so we could be closer, and she could "get to know her grandkids." We wrote a lot of letters to each other during those years, and once again she told me she needed help in figuring out what I was calling our seemingly empty relationship. In the next sentence, she said, "I need you to tell me specifically what you want from me." In essence, she made it my problem, and believe me I gave her a specific list of several ways I felt we could improve things between us. Somewhere the ball would get dropped and we'd be right back where we started.

There would be many years of back and forth and up and down before I would finally settle on, "Abbi face it, your mother is unable to give you what you need and want, LET IT GO!"

And I'd be fine for a while and then young Abbi would stir up inside and I'd get triggered by some family event and I'd let her have it, trying one more time: "Like, really Mom, I'm not asking for anything out of the ordinary, am I?"

CHAPTER 9

Fifth Generation Farm Gals

*"What doesn't kill you makes you stronger. Learn from the past.
Each opportunity, good or bad is an opportunity to learn."*

~Author Unknown

I gave myself permission to look at inheriting the family farm as a sort of compensation for years of pain and suffering we endured while growing up. When it became evident that my father's illness was terminal, his doctors suggested he get his affairs in order and he involved all four of us girls in the meetings with attorneys and his accountant.

I soon learned that passing a farming business to the next generation – especially one with two thousand acres of land worth four thousand dollars an acre – was quite the tricky deal. There were a host of legalities to be sorted out, not to mention the potential inheritance tax consequences. After a somewhat lengthy process a plan for passing the farm down to the next generation was in place.

Under normal circumstances my mother's interests would have been part of the calculations as well; however, when they divorced my father had warned her against trying to claim her rightful portion of the farm. She obeyed and walked away from the twenty-five-year marriage with a place to live in Denver and that was pretty much it. But she did have her sanity, and for that she was forever grateful!

My father had incurred a fair amount of debt over the years (pretty typical in the farming industry), which was then handed down to my three sisters and me. There was also a solid plan in place to whittle the debt down over a twenty-year period, and so it made sense, given the value of the real estate, to take it on. The attorneys had also elected for "special use tax," which was beneficial but also required us to actively farm the land for ten years before we could divide it.

The four of us, along with our spouses, got together to figure out what made the most sense, given our present circumstances and lifestyles. Terri, as mentioned, was running her law firm in Denver, five hundred miles away; Kurt and I lived thirty miles away and were running our own farm operation, which Kurt had been involved in with his family when we married. It was decided that Heidi and Jenni and their husbands would farm the ground, while Terri and I would weigh in on important decisions. Jenni would also handle most of the bookkeeping, while I served as secretary at our monthly meetings. We called our business venture "Four Sisters."

This system worked fairly well for several years, but eventually communication started to breakdown, which was hurtful and caused stress and angst for everyone; it also led to some trust issues. We had been thrust into a family business with no experience in making group decisions, each of us trying to take everyone's perspective into consideration, in addition to our own agendas. As is the case with most things in life there are many ways to run a business, and we each seemed to have different ideas about how to go about it. Dad was no longer there running the show and by God, we were each going to stand up and be counted! It was the moment we had all been waiting for, the ability to have an opinion and a voice to speak it.

That's where it got a bit sticky, and Rick Hammond, Heidi's husband, often found himself in the middle.

Rick, who we affectionately called "Ricardo," had a good handle on the farm operation, and fielded many phone calls where a couple of us often demanded, "Where's the money?"

Rick took our requests to heart and did everything in his power to find programs that would improve our operation, such as cost-share for pivot drops that made watering our crops more efficient. He was bold and courageous and convinced us to sign up almost two-quarters of the farm ground into a water conservation project. It was a government program where landowners enrolled the land in a hundred-year easement, with the intention to put it back to its native landscape. It netted us quite a nice sum of money, and today the wetlands are planted mostly to native grasses and the cattle are able to graze there.

This project actually undid one of Dad's visions for the basin ground. He had tirelessly fought against Mother Nature on a variety of occasions, almost all of them involving trying to control water. Back in the '70s he had spent countless hours sitting on the D8 caterpillar, bought for this sole purpose, hoping to transform basin ground into irrigated farm ground. He literally moved tons of dirt and built a huge dam a quarter mile long on all three sides. He created a body of water that covered several acres, which enabled him to farm several small patches of the two quarters and allowed us to irrigate the crops from the water in the basin with large pumps run by tractors. According to today's practices it wouldn't be considered an economical way to farm, but my father saw it as one of his most interesting projects he undertook when he was at the helm.

Just a side note here – dirt found in basin areas is usually quite dense and very sticky when wet, and one can just imagine what it was like for us girls when it rained, and we had to set the pumps to pull the water off the fields and pump it into the dam. I clearly remember a day when a tractor got caught in the muck and Heidi proceeded to get four more tractors stuck trying to pull it out! It was just one more occasion when a diesel-powered tow truck traveled out from the city to get the folks of the Harrington farmstead out of a jam.

Eventually, differing agendas among the sisters led to a breakdown, to the point where Rick and I felt that in order to prevent long-lasting damage to our family relationship it was time to seek professional help. To their credit, while not all of my sisters agreed with this suggestion, they honored the request. This act of generosity and kindness says a lot about who they are as humans, and I am forever grateful to them.

We hired Carolyn Rodenberg from End Conflict, a consulting business in Kansas that specialized in working with farm families. Carolyn explained that a lack of clear communication from the father was common in many families while the children were growing up, with the father unwilling to admit that there were problems and stressors. Farmers in particular tended to hold things close and not share them with family members, which projected a false image to the neighbors who were sometimes seen as competitors.

While I respected Carolyn's input, it was my experience that my father *did* share his stressors. Unfortunately, he did this by erupting into major temper tantrums, throwing tools or beating on a cow or whatever else he could get his hands on. Of course, to go along with the tantrum was an entire string of obnoxious expletives.

There were also stressors outside the farm. My father had a passion for trading stocks and commodities, but he often made impulsive decisions that yielded frustrating, if not scary, results. I recall many times when he put the whole family on alert, announcing, "We are in dire straits, there will be no more spending money for a while."

Then one day things would magically be back to normal and he'd be off on his next project, which left me wondering, "So, is our financial situation better?"

Our first meeting with Carolyn took place in the conference room of a local hotel. She began by meeting with each of us one-on-one, for the purpose of gathering information and making sure everyone's voice was heard. When it became evident to her that there were issues between two parties, she would call them both into the room to get it out in the open and offer suggestions of how to resolve it. She was highly talented, knowing exactly the right questions to ask, and actively listening to each individual's responses. It was a powerful process that really did help us figure out how to continue working together. For this I was thankful, as I had lots of guilt and shame around requesting professional assistance and felt I bore responsibility for the process. I felt like the "bad sister," the troublemaker, and certainly the black sheep of the family. I've since noticed that these feelings of guilt and shame often surface when it comes to dealing with my family.

I often asked myself, "Why can't I just let things be?"

Carolyn described our family situation as "severe." After meeting with each of us she concluded, "Your father never grew up. He threw tantrums and you girls were at stake. Your mother decided not to confront your father and just shrugged her shoulders and said, "Oh well, nothing I can do about it."

Carolyn recalled the physical and emotional abuse we suffered at the hands of our father and called it out for what it was – inexcusable.

In subsequent meetings, Carolyn worked on teaching us how to be better communicators. She explained the process called "triangulating," where two people talk about a third person without that person present for the conversation. Unfortunately, this was happening a lot and was creating stress for everyone. From Carolyn we learned that when we found ourselves in this particular situation we should ask, "Have you talked with them?" Usually, the answer was no. The next question was, "Can you talk to them?" Once again, the answer was usually No. The final question to ask was, "Would you like me to go with you to talk with them?" to which the answer was usually yes, unless the person was just venting and then it became a nonissue. This was a very useful tool for all of us and is something all families can use to communicate in a more honest manner with each other.

Over a period of two years, Carolyn facilitated several of our business meetings, and she taught us how to utilize "Consensus Tally" when voting on an agenda item. The options for voting were: 1, meaning "I'm on board 100%"; 2, meaning "I'm not 100% but I won't badmouth the decision"; or 3, meaning, "No, we need to look at other options." This little tool was absolutely amazing and brought us more success than any other.

While it was gratifying to be in the farming business with my family and learn how to honor each other's perspective, after thirteen years I was ready to move on. One particular fall day before harvest, me, my sisters and our spouses gathered in the living room of the house we grew up in. Carolyn was there to facilitate the meeting. We had worked all morning on some projects and we now had to make some decisions about whether we were to stay together and move forward. I wasn't feeling it, and though I was scared I knew I needed to speak up. When we took the vote Terri, Heidi, and Jenni all voted a strong "1," – meaning we should stay together and keep moving forward." When it was my turn to vote I said, "I vote a 3," meaning "we need to look at other options. I then burst into tears.

Another tool Carolyn taught us was to learn to be "gut-level honest" with each other. What that entailed for me was to dig down deep inside and listen to that inner voice that I had shut off so many years ago.

It took all my strength to say, "I'm done." Me, the silent one, the mouse in the corner who took in all the crazy family dynamics for all those years. Being in business with my sisters made it too challenging to shake those old family patterns that had been so deeply ingrained in me. And I realized that after all these years the farm represented so much pain and agony for me, so many memories growing up that filled me with trauma. Though I appreciated the legacy Dad had left us, I just couldn't do it any longer.

The way Carolyn expressed it, "The farm and family represented one big ugly bundle for you."

Once I voted a 3, Rick stood and said, "This will be the best for all of us." I don't recall my sisters saying anything. Very little was ever said to me and to this day I still sometimes wonder what they were thinking. I do remember Terri returning to Denver and telling me she would call me when she could stop crying, which took seven days. I also recall the guilt and shame I felt for splitting up the Four Sisters farming business.

Thus, began the monumental task of valuing the farm ground, equipment, buildings, and houses. We leaned on the husbands to do this part, and they worked diligently to come up with a good plan. We each received approximately three quarters of farm ground, while the buildings and grain bins were divided amongst the three of them as I had no desire for any of those things. I also no longer had a share in our family home where many memories still loomed large. My three sisters then continued the business under its new name, "Three Sisters."

I know Dad wanted the farm to stay together after he passed, and it had for thirteen solid years. Even after I left, the farm remained in the family, and it still does to this day.

At the end of 2019, I sold my last piece of farm ground to my niece and her husband, officially making it a sixth-generation family farm. The deal was an investment not only in their future, but mine and Kurt's as well. With the proceeds I was able to purchase one hundred sixty acres of farm ground in the area where we live so we get to actively farm it. A win for both parties!

PART II

Coming Home to Me, 2020

CHAPTER 10

The Fight of My Life: Keystone Pipeline

"Never doubt that a small group of thoughtful, committed citizens can change the world. In fact, it is the only thing that ever has."

~Margaret Mead

In my wildest dreams, I never would have imagined that a proposed pipeline would wake me up to the life I was supposed to be living. It makes sense now; as a female, mother and nurturer of my family, I could not stand idly by while a foreign corporation known as TransCanada wanted to rape our farm ground with a toxic pipeline and put our land and water at risk. Perhaps, it also awakened some dormant passion for advocacy passed down to me by my father. Whatever the case, engaging in this "fight of my life" was the impetus that allowed me to begin to step fully into my power and unleash the true self burning inside of me, yearning to be free.

It began in September of 2013, with a phone call from my niece Meghan. "Hey, Aunt Abbi, they came out with the new proposed route of the pipeline today and it looks like it runs through your farmland." She said the words matter-of-factly, while on the other end of the line my mouth hung open in disbelief.

"No, it doesn't, Meghan. You are just joking, there's no way!"

"Well, as best as Dad and I can tell that's what it looks like from the map."

Once again, I replied with, "Meghan, there's just no way, I don't believe you."

She emailed me the new map and I saw for myself that the new proposed route of the Keystone pipeline snaked right through our family farm. I had previously heard about the pipeline because the first proposed route went through Heidi and Rick's property, which was twenty miles north of the farm. In fact, Rick had told me several times what a tough time he was having with the TransCanada land agent who repeatedly knocked on their door. The guy, who doubled as a Baptist preacher, pulled out all the stops in trying to get them to agree. First, he tried to sell them on the deal, offering a generous one-time sum of money in exchange for granting TransCanada indefinite access to their farm ground. If Rick and Heidi didn't agree, he threatened, their land would be taken by force, through eminent domain.

Heidi would have nothing to do with the guy. Her take was, "That's what husbands are for."

Unsure what to do, Rick contacted his attorney, who said, "There's not much you *can* do but agree to it."

So Rick and Heidi begrudgingly signed the paperwork only to learn a year later that the company had changed the route. Their relief was short-lived though, because the new route included two quarters of the farm ground they farmed on our family farm. If TransCanada had only known this was the case, I assure you they would have veered off in another direction, rather than deal with Rick's resistance again!

At this news an enormous amount of fear arose from within me, for several logical reasons. First, while I had heard of eminent domain, I was unaware that a foreign corporation could simply come in and take our land. Eminent domain is used when the project is for public gain within the country. There would be no public gain from this pipeline, only further destruction from climate change that was already occurring at a maddening pace. My ancestors had shed too much blood, sweat, and tears to keep the land in the family for me to even consider such a deal.

Secondly, this pipeline was no ordinary pipeline. The pipe was going to be three feet in diameter – which is considered quite large – and only buried three feet underneath the soil. It wasn't like they were planning to bury the pipeline in a right-of-way like a ditch or the edge of the field either; they were going right down the middle of the field! If a farm implement happened to hit the pipeline and cause damage, the farmer would be responsible for repairing it. To make matters worse, the substance they were going to pump through the pipeline was a tar-like, toxic substance called bitumen, a byproduct of petroleum. Spills would cause quite a mess, which the farmer would also have to clean up at his expense. We learned that this end-product would go out to the open market and more than likely China would buy it. It wasn't even for our country!

In Nebraska, we are blessed with an underground water supply known as the Ogallala Aquifer. It was never a question of if the pipeline would leak its toxic crap into the aquifer, but when. The pipeline was also going to have to cross many rivers and streams as it made its way to the refineries in the Gulf of Mexico. I can only imagine the stand my father would have taken had he been alive, but I can assure you he was with us in spirit.

As if TransCanada's threat was not enough, one afternoon a random fire ignited a few miles south of our house, sending up smoke that could be seen for miles. Once again, I experienced an intense out-of-control feeling as I watched that fire race cross country, devouring whatever was in its path. That unexplained fire was also part of my wakeup call.

Most of the crops had been harvested by that time, but the fire was fed by grass and corn stubble, outbuildings, and pivot tires. It would eventually burn several hundred acres, but all the people and homes were spared thanks to the magical work of our angels, some in spirit and others in the bodies of firefighters. I remembered a movie my sister had recently mentioned to me, about how life as we know it would end with a massive fire burning us up. That stuck in my mind and I began experiencing all kinds of strange physical sensations in my body, one of which was a constant ringing in my ears. The ENT doctor I saw could find nothing wrong and said it was probably from all the smoke; the MRI he ordered showed only some inflammation. Intuitively I knew different, but I'll delve more into this later.

A week later I headed to New York City with my two daughters-in-law for some sightseeing and shopping. Unfortunately, we arrived shortly before the much-anticipated Hurricane Sandy and after three days of fun it became quite evident that we needed to hightail it out of there or risk getting stuck in the city. We had been keeping a watchful eye on the forecast, but it was when our cab driver started talking about flooded subways and trapped people that we made our decision. We canceled our return flight, which was scheduled to leave Monday morning, then headed to La Guardia Airport where we planned to rent a car, drive to Pittsburgh, and catch a flight from there. It was all divine timing, as many other people had the same idea and the line at the Hertz car rental was long. Luckily, my daughter-in-law had a gold club membership and we were able to proceed quickly to the front of the line. Once in the car and high on adrenaline, we drove seven hours through the night to Pittsburgh, where we got a hotel room so we could sleep for a few short hours before our flights. We were so grateful to have made it out, especially when we saw what a number Hurricane Sandy did to the city! Global warming certainly had my attention, and the hurricane also triggered some trauma from my childhood days, when my father was the "uncontrollable storm" in my life.

Both Mother Nature and TransCanada were showing me how much control I *didn't* have, and this had my fears escalating. However, as always, there were blessings to be found amidst the challenges. The organization BOLD Nebraska was one of those blessings, becoming our sounding board and safety net where the pipeline was concerned. They would help us "circle our wagons" to protect the land and water that was both our history and our livelihood.

I remember the first time I met Jane Kleeb, the founder and voice of BOLD Nebraska. Jane was this spunky, passionate, encouraging, intelligent woman who from the very beginning helped me feel empowered and reassured by her confident presence. By the time my family and I joined BOLD Nebraska, Jane and her fellow activists were already seasoned warriors in the fight against TransCanada, having worked with the farmers and ranchers in the Sandhills along the initial proposed route. The members of this well-oiled machine were highly adept, creative, and had their ducks in a row, always strategizing and ready to push back. As a family used to keeping its problems in-house, we were learning the value of coming together with our fellow travelers when dealing with an issue such as this.

Before TransCanada could split the gut of our country open with their pipeline, they had to obtain a federal permit. The State Department held hearings in several different locations, one of which was Albion, Nebraska. Though I was afraid of the pipeline, and rather skeptical that anything could be done about it, I decided, at Rick and Meghan's insistence, to ride along with them to the meeting.

As we drove onto the fairgrounds that evening there were a half dozen large tour buses and I asked Rick, "What in the heck are those buses doing here?"

Rick replied, "TransCanada buses in pipefitters who will testify in favor of building the pipeline as it is their way of living."

"How clever of them," I said sarcastically.

The fairgrounds parking lot was quite full, and we had to stand in line to register for the meeting. By the time we got inside and found seats in front, folks in favor of the pipeline were already speaking. Instantly I became angry and couldn't wait for them to finish so those of us in opposition could present. However, when their allotted five minutes was up, they were replaced by others who also supported the pipeline. This continued for what felt like an eternity.

I turned to Rick and said, "What the hell is this about, why are they all speaking in favor of the pipeline?"

Calmly, Rick replied, "Oh, that is a ploy that TransCanada uses. They get here first and fill the signup sheet with all the pipefitters and folks who have agreed to speak in favor of it, hopefully influencing the State Department to approve the project."

I was livid, and growing increasingly annoyed by Rick and Meghan, who were "shushing" me, nudging me and whispering, "Quiet down or they will throw you out!"

Finally, I got up and walked to the back of the room, searching for a friendly face. That's when I noticed a gentleman leaning against the wall. He was dressed in hiking gear with a rather large backpack by his side. Without giving it too much thought I walked up to him, reached out my hand and introduced myself. I then asked him what he was doing at the meeting.

He introduced himself as Ken Illgunas and he told me he was walking the entire length of the proposed Keystone pipeline, beginning in Fort McMurray, Alberta, Canada. The boreal forest was being destroyed for the mining of bitumen, which was what was going to flow through the pipeline. Mining the bitumen took incredible amounts of water and fuel; it also left in its wake a landscape dotted with enormous "tailings ponds," which were basically lifeless gray seas of leftover sludge. Ken had also flown over the area to get a more comprehensive perspective of the devastation to the environment.

He was headed seventeen hundred miles south to Port Arthur, Texas, where the bitumen would be refined and sent out to the world market.

After that enlightening conversation I introduced Rick and Meghan to him, and Rick advised him on which path he might follow while walking through our neck of the woods. It wasn't but a few days later when Rick was coming back from the sale barn in Fullerton and he spotted a person in the ditch, sitting there resting with full gear on his back. Sure enough, it was Ken, and Rick convinced him to come and stay at our farm. Ken accepted his offer but refused to get into a gas-powered vehicle while hiking the path of the pipeline, as this was his way of taking a stand. The next day Rick met Ken several miles north of the farm with horses, which they rode while Meghan hauled Ken's gear in the back of the pickup.

It wasn't too difficult to convince Ken to stay a few extra days at our farmhouse. He had some writing to do and was going to map out the next leg of his journey, plus it was a particularly cold January. He was a wonderful guest, and an entertaining one, sharing some pretty wild stories. One that stands out for me took place in a small town in northern Nebraska. Ken was eating at a convenience store when a sheriff came up to him and told him he'd been instructed to take Ken out of the county. The locals weren't used to seeing guys like Ken, and they were suspicious that he might be responsible for a couple of house break-ins that afternoon. Ken tried to reassure him he was just a good guy on an expedition to Texas, walking the route of the proposed pipeline. Ken even told the sheriff he could search his backpack, but the sheriff insisted Ken needed to leave and he was going to drive him out of the county. Ken wasn't too happy about breaking his vow not to ride in a gas-powered vehicle but since he also didn't care to get arrested, he had no choice.

When it came time to head south along the pipeline route again, Rick decided it would be a kind gesture to walk with Ken, at least for a few miles. A few miles turned to sixty miles before he called it quits because he felt he was slowing Ken down. Needless to say, walking sixty miles in January with heavy gear on your back is a pretty nice show of support, and I'm sure Ken enjoyed the company and conversation.

Nineteen hundred miles and one hundred and thirty-six days after leaving Alberta, Ken arrived in Port Arthur and headed for the Valero refinery.

As he got closer, he was assaulted by a smell he described as, "A cauldron of chemicals, a bonfire put out by a gallon of Windex. My tongue began to tingle, so I tried my best not to swallow."

He also took a series of photos, which irritated the locals patrolling the area. He was stopped by several police officers, one of whom told him not to take any more photos.

When he had finished his surveillance, he sprinted across the steep bridge and put his feet in Sabine Lake, which empties into the Gulf of Mexico, to signal the end of his journey. Ken wrote an amazing book describing his experiences entitled, "Trespassing Across America."

CHAPTER 11

Arrest at the White House

"Protest beyond the law is not a departure from democracy;
it is absolutely essential to it."

~Howard Zinn

By the time my family and I joined the ongoing pushback against the pipeline many national groups like the Sierra Club, 360.org and CREDO were already onboard, planning and organizing protests all over the country. With a boldness that would have surely done my father proud, I agreed to be arrested for civil disobedience in front of the White House. In January of 2014, I along with my sister Jenni and my niece Meghan traveled with BOLD Nebraska to Washington D.C. for the protest and to meet with State Department officials and our Nebraska representatives.

I soon learned that being part of a protest, when organized by an experienced advocacy group, is quite different from what we might see on TV. In our case, the details had already been worked out with the D.C. Park Police so everyone was aware of the parameters and exactly how the protest would work. They also provided civil disobedience training for those being arrested. Other groups were protesting that day as well, including climate activists gathered in a park near the arresting sight. Bobby Kennedy Jr. had joined them, and he spoke of how vital it was that Americans protect our land and water, especially from a ruthless, foreign corporation.

Jenni was deeply moved by Bobby's passionate words. "Who is that guy?" she asked, then kept repeating, "Listen to what he is saying, he gets it!"

I knew at that moment that Jenni was in the fight for the long haul.

At the appointed time, forty-five climate change activists and three Nebraska farmers headed for the north side of the White House. I didn't know it at the time, but also being arrested were several prominent people including Sierra Club CEO Michael Brune; Bill McKibben from 360.org; Kenny Bruno from Greenpeace; and hip-hop organizer Reverend Lennox Yearwood Jr.

The D.C. Park Police told us where to stand; they also had barricades that kept the media in place. Then, while our group was posing for a photo for the news media, I heard a woman's voice from behind me say, "They can't see me."

The next thing I knew, I was being directed to move to the front row, so the mysterious woman was visible to the reporters. Imagine my surprise when I turned around to see none other than Daryl Hannah! I found this a bit humorous but understood why it was important for a Hollywood actress to be visible in the photographs. She would certainly draw more attention to the cause than a farmer from Nebraska!

After we'd stood for fifteen or twenty minutes the police announced that we either needed to move or we would be under arrest. All of us who had agreed to be arrested stayed put, the police handcuffed us and began leading us one-by-one to nearby "paddy wagons," where we were instructed to get in the back. I ended up sitting right next to Daryl Hannah and Cherrie Foylin, a well-known activist from Louisiana. She works with the Indigenous tribes from her area who suffer many health issues as a result of the pollution from the oil refineries located in the Gulf of Mexico.

The police officers drove us to the holding area at Anacostia Park along the Potomac River, where we were ticketed and placed, still in handcuffs, in a holding cell for about thirty minutes. Once everyone had been processed the police began releasing us, and that was that. As we walked out to freedom, other pipeline fighters, including Jenni and Meghan, were there to greet us. To Jenni's delight, we even got the chance to say thank you to Bobby Kennedy Jr. as he and his teenage son, who were also arrested, were leaving.

The next day the contingency from Nebraska, including organizer Jane Kleeb, met with eight individuals at the State Department for an hour. They were extremely attentive, took notes, and asked us questions about the project. We informed them that we had seen the report about the benefits of the pipeline, and now we needed to see a report about the detriment to the environment caused by the pipeline.

We also met with our representation from Nebraska, who were nothing short of rude. They showed little interest in hearing any position contrary to theirs, which was that the project was in the country's best interests. For me, the final straw was when one of the senators shouted to our group, "I will not talk tar sands!" That's when I walked out of the meeting room. On the other hand, we were fortunate to visit with Senator Sheldon Whitehouse of Rhode Island. He was right with us and totally supported our cause, which was much appreciated after our less-than-positive visit with our fellow Nebraskans.

On Sunday we participated in the largest climate rally march ever held in the United States. It was like nothing I had ever experienced before and though it was a bitterly cold day we stayed warm from the enthusiasm of the crowd. That day, an estimated thirty-five thousand people marched through the streets of D.C. chanting, "This is what democracy looks like!"

Another chant was, "Hey, hey, ho, ho, Keystone pipeline has got to go!" We ended up gathering in the open space at the Washington Monument, where many speakers, some of whom I had been arrested with, shared their concerns about the Keystone pipeline and climate change in general.

We were in Washington D.C. for six days, accomplished a lot and I felt quite empowered and hopeful when I returned home. I look back on the experience as the initial spark that woke me up to life. I was continuing to remember that I had a voice that I could use to say how I felt and what I believed. There will always be naysayers – that is part of life. For the longest time it was so important for me to fit in and belong, and I felt that if I participated in activism I would be shunned. I'm now willing to embrace what I am passionate about and not worry about what other people think.

In May of that same year, 2013, the State Department held a hearing in Grand Island, Nebraska, at which I was to speak. As luck would have it, Mother Nature surprised us with an all-out spring blizzard that morning, but if anything, this only made me more determined to get there. My sister Terri had traveled from Colorado to attend the hearing with me, and we began the hour-long, precarious drive before daylight. Nothing was going to stop me from having my say, not even when we had to back up on the interstate and take another route because of an accident ahead! My sister and I finally made it to the fairgrounds in Grand Island and then proceeded to stand in line outside in the cold and snow for a couple of hours before we could get into the auditorium where we would be speaking.

Like the protest in D.C., it was a very unifying and empowering experience. Terri and I, along with other family members were part of a large group of pipeline fighters, all sitting together and wearing matching t-shirts. When it was my turn to speak, I addressed the risks to our land and water, saying that this pipeline was not for the greater good of the American people, and that no foreign corporation was coming in to take the land that had been in my family for five generations.

In between pipeline meetings and courtroom hearings our pipeline fighting group also spent time at the state capital, testifying on the eminent domain bill and others that came before committee hearings. We didn't have too much support from our state leaders but that didn't stop us from sharing our valid concerns. We also held several rallies on the steps of the capital and marched around downtown Lincoln in protest of the pipeline.

That next summer we focused our cause at the county level, as York County had no zoning regulations on oil pipelines. We spent months working tirelessly to convince the board of county commissioners, but everything we said fell on deaf ears. We never did get York County to enact any zoning regulations, and we speculated that the commissioners had been bought and sold by big oil. I know I wondered more than once if things might have been different with a woman on the board.

The fight went on, however, with far more victories than defeats. Jane Kleeb continued to lead our organizing efforts, and our attorneys; Dave Domina and Brian Jorde did a spectacular job representing the landowners in court, winning nearly every judgment. Then Jane and company came up with the unique idea to build a renewable energy barn along the proposed path, and Terri agreed to allow it on a corner of her farm ground.

It was an amazing experience. We had an old-fashioned barn raising, with pipeline fighters showing up in droves to help us build it. The christening of the barn was a mighty celebration, with philanthropist, environmentalist, and activist Tom Steyer flying in from California to do the honors. It was one of the windiest days in memory, but it did not deter a large crowd from gathering to listen to his impassioned speech and take part in the festivities. Local firefighters came a couple of times to wet down the dirt, but everyone had dirt in their ears and eyes by the end of the day.

Our intention was to send a very clear message to President Barack Obama: "You will have to tear down clean energy to put a dirty tar sands pipeline in our soil!" And it must have worked, because in November of 2014, our most honorable president REJECTED THE KEYSTONE PIPELINE! When you "circle your wagons," amazing things do happen!

Unfortunately, the pipeline was revived when Donald Trump was elected in 2016, and though it wasn't built during his term it remained a constant threat. There were still some lawsuits pending, which was a good thing because we knew the longer the pipeline was delayed the less likely it would ever be built. In the meantime, Jane persisted as our fearless leader and we remained as determined as ever to beat this thing once and for all, however long it took.

On January 20, 2021, President Joe Biden's first day in office, he signed an executive action stopping further construction of the Keystone pipeline. God bless our democracy! I do declare, I am awake and aware! A large celebration is planned for all who pushed back against TransCanada at Rick and Heidi's luxurious barn event center in 2021 – after the pandemic, of course.

CHAPTER 12

The Invitation

"Our deepest fear is not that we are inadequate. Our deepest fear is that we are powerful beyond measure. It is our light, not our darkness that frightens us. Your playing small does not serve the world."

~Marianne Williamson

I've come to realize that we eventually receive the messages we need to hear, even if we aren't consciously aware of them at the time. I admit that when my sister Terri sent the above quote to me about ten years ago, it didn't hold much meaning for me. Yet I hung it inside the laundry room cupboard, where I would see it every time I opened the door to get cleaning supplies. It was as if there was some vague awareness of an unconscious energy that needed to be explored. I know now that I had been playing small most of my life and accepting that message on a conscious level would have meant I had to do something about it. I thought I'd experienced enough discomfort and challenges and had decided that I was just going to stay comfortable. Looking back, I now know that when I hung that message it was because my higher self knew at some point, I would be ready to see the truth. Grace is a good thing.

The fact that my Higher Self chose to hang the quote inside my cleaning supply cupboard is also significant. It spoke to a decision I had made many years earlier, that I could gain self-worth from keeping a spotless home (yes, I used to vacuum the garage). It was as if I was determined to embody the phrase "cleanliness is next to Godliness," though in my case "cleanliness is next to worthiness" might have been more accurate.

This seemed to be validated by an insurance salesman, who commented, "You are the kind of customer we like to see. I can tell by looking at your home you run a tight ship."

Though he meant that as a compliment, something about his words struck a chord. They alerted me to the fact that I had been choosing to play small. I knew having a clean house gave me a sense of control; it was one uncluttered space in a life dominated by my mind chatter. In other words, it brought me comfort, which was something I craved so much while growing up.

Things really started to shift in August of 2019, when my youngest son left for college (he had planned to go to the local university, but changed his mind and decided to attend a school fifteen hundred miles away!). I had already been doing inner work for many years, but now I gave myself permission to focus fully on "coming home to me." I wasn't sure what that would look like but I knew it was time.

It was during this part of my journey that I realized I was ready to let the tidy house syndrome go in favor of more fun, creative activities (like writing this book) I knew were possible. These days, my house is still pretty clean but it certainly is not the priority it had been for so many years. I have heard creative people say that their workspace has to be rather messy for their right brain to work effectively. Since I started writing I have noticed that the desks and floor of my writing space can easily get piled high with books and papers. This no longer makes me feel cluttered or confined; instead, it reminds me that the possibilities are endless!

I can look up at a dirty ceiling fan and say, "Oh my, will you take a look at that dust?" and keep right on going.

I have decided that things like dog hair floating around as I type and dirty windows are things that make you say, "What's not to love about that?"

That is where I am now, and it is wonderful. Getting to this point, however, was very painful and required a fortitude I never knew I possessed. When Cameron left for school I had been parenting for thirty-six years and was used to putting my kids' needs and desires before my own a good majority of the time. In fact, it had become second nature. (I kid you not, for years when I listened to flight attendants say, "Be sure to secure your oxygen mask before assisting others," I would be like, *Honey, you've got that back-ward! Your kid's mask always comes before yours!* Some lessons take longer to learn than others.)

As I was well aware by this point, recognizing a pattern is a great first step; however, changing it would take some time; a conscious aware-ness; and likely some kind of professional guidance. Indeed, during the fall of 2019, I found myself in deep emotional turmoil, desperately grieving the fact that I could no longer see and care for my son as I had every day for eighteen years. It didn't help that his decision to move away came about suddenly (fall football camp was starting in just a few days and if he was going to join the team he needed to go), which meant none of us had time to really process it. On a deeper level, I believe Cameron's higher self knew that if he was going to become a successful young man he was going to have to get out from under Mom's wing and learn to fly on his own.

I was worried about his well-being, not only because he was so far away from home, but because over the years I had picked up on all the fears looming large in the world where Black people's safety is concerned. It made the natural instinct all mothers have to protect their children go into overdrive.

The depths of my despair and fear after his departure alerted me to the fact that I was at a major crossroads in my life. After a lifetime of caring for and protecting others, the only person I had to "save" was myself! It began when I made the brave and courageous choice to look at myself in the mirror and ask, "Now what are you going to do? The time has come; you are an empty-nester."

There were many days when I didn't think I would survive. Heidi, my sweet sister and earth angel, was always there to lovingly remind me, "You are stronger than you know, and you will survive!" Other times, Gloria Gaynor came to my rescue. I would command Alexa to play, "I Will Survive," then turn up the volume and dance. Somedays I still do!

And on the days I didn't believe I would survive because I was so full of fear, I would get down on my knees and tearfully beg my higher power, "Please, please, please help me! Please keep Cameron safe."

During this time of transition, my dear husband was my "stable steady rock," as I refer to him. Kurt seldom wavers on the outside. He has always allowed me the freedom to work my process and I know he has my back, as I have his.

Author and human potential thought leader Bryant McGill has said, "Our children can be our greatest teachers if we are humble enough to receive their lessons." This has certainly been the case with Cam, though the lessons are quite uncomfortable and at times painful. He has brightly shone a light on places within me that have been begging for healing. I came to realize recently that my need to protect him and keep him safe was in part left over from my own childhood, when I had to figure out how to feel safe on my own. Cam is so well-protected and loved by Spirit, angels, and earthly people that there is no way he will not thrive in this lifetime. It took me nineteen years to figure out that I am not his protector and that it's not my job to keep him safe. I'm not that powerful. I often tap into my Dad's spirit and ask him to guide Cameron. I know Dad thinks Cameron is an amazing young man!

Through this experience, I have learned the truth of Heidi's words – we are all so much more resilient than we ever allow ourselves to even imagine. I have also come to understand that in our weakest moments we are the strongest, even when it feels like we are completely broken. When we are broken open by the ups and downs of life, it is from this place that we get back up, dust ourselves off, and see the whole world anew. It is in times of deep turmoil we learn to tap into the Divine Spirit that lives within us and allow that very powerful energy to lift and guide us to what is for the highest good of all, trusting that goodness abounds and we will be taken care of.

"Life is amazing. And then it's awful.
And then it's amazing again.
And in between the amazing and the awful
It's ordinary and mundane and routine.
Breathe in the amazing.
Hold on through the awful,
And relax and exhale during the ordinary.
That's just living.
Heartbreaking, soul-healing,
Amazing, awful, ordinary life.
And it's breathtakingly beautiful."

~L.R. Knost

CHAPTER 13

Making Myself a Priority

"It takes courage to endure the sharp pains of self-discovery rather than choose to take the dull pain of unconsciousness that would last the rest of our lives."

~Marianne Williamson

A s I was exploring the idea of harnessing my inner power the word "empowerment" popped up in my mind. I became curious, and as I was searching for a definition of the word, I was serendipitously led to an article entitled "Authentically Empowered," by personal transformation life coach specialist Donna Bond. "To feel authentically empowered," she wrote, "is to feel safe and secure in who you are and what you know to be true for you. It is also a state of inner authority." When I read those words, I knew I had been reunited with my truth; my heart and soul were in total agreement. From this place of authentic oneness, we are open to all of the gifts life has to offer and wants to give us. That moment of realization is forever etched in my memory as the ticket back to my true self.

I also drew from the wisdom of other thought leaders, including positive psychologist Dr. Robert Holden. "No amount of self-improvement,"

Holden stated, "can make up for the lack of self-acceptance." I also reso-
nated with these words from life coach Brooke Castillo: "You can never
out-perform your self-image."

I became aware, perhaps for the first time, that loving and accepting myself
unconditionally was the starting point for all future transformations to
occur. This has been my biggest stumbling block by far and I was so grateful
to finally have the missing piece to the puzzle.

Gary Zuzak defines authentic empowerment as "the alignment of the personality with the soul: what it involves, how it happens, and what it creates.
When the energy of the soul is recognized, acknowledged, and valued, it
begins to infuse the life of the personality."

My personality had hijacked my Higher Self over the years. I was holding
on for dear life and not allowing the two parts to work in tandem and be
a team. When we are empowered, we have the freedom to live heart-centered lives which are much more expansive, free, and life-giving. We are also
capable of including the ego's needs, so it doesn't have to fight for control.
Life stops being a struggle and becomes a journey, an adventure with one
discovery leading to another. Recognizing and letting go of limiting beliefs
is also required for the journey to my authentic, empowered self.

There is a popular saying in spiritual circles: "The teacher appears when the
student is ready." Many times, the teacher also shows up *before* the student
is ready and as I've painstakingly learned, that's okay also. I do believe in
perfect timing and I also believe that when we try to force something to
happen a certain way in a particular time frame, we are asking for continued
struggle. We must learn to love our humanness. We get it when we get it.
Our truths come when we are ready for them.

Realizing my authentic empowered self was within reach came with such
jubilation and joy! My Higher Self had been so patient and knew things
were in alignment for transformation to begin. I lovingly embrace the

serendipitous moments that happen when I am one with life. I am content knowing that I am right on time, without a doubt!

At the end of Donna Bond's article, the reader was invited to reach out to her if they had a desire to explore the concept of authentic empowerment more fully. Shortly after I submitted the online survey provided, my phone rang. I contemplated not answering it, but my intuition spoke louder than my fearful self. As soon as I heard the friendly voice on the other end, I knew I had made the right decision.

That said, I began my spiritual psychology coaching journey with transformational life coach, Donna Bond with some trepidation. There was a lot for me to uncover and let go of and I knew life was about to shift, change, and get a lot more uncomfortable once again. It became evident early on in our work together that there was a clear distinction between the curriculum Donna offered and what other therapists or coaches I had experience with, were utilizing. Spiritual psychology is the study and practice of the art and science of conscious awakening, which includes the vital practice of self-forgiveness.

Our higher power has unconditional love for us, and it resides within each of us, always. That said, we have to be willing to embody that love to transmute all the patterns of behavior that aren't for our highest good. That message was clear as a bell ringing on a crisp, blue-sky, see-your-breath kind of morning! Self-love and self-compassion are my guiding lights on this journey. That I know for certain.

I had studied lots of spiritual teachings through the years, and while I gained new knowledge from all of them, I hadn't learned to embody the new information to fully step into my authentically empowered self. It was Donna who taught me that when we fail to transmute patterns of behavior that are no longer serving our highest good and replace them with our true loving essence, we simply fall back into the familiar. By loving the human self, I am better able to tap into my spiritual self.

Even though my Higher Self knew what was for my highest good, my ego-self had almost always won out because it was the louder voice inside of me. My ego had been leading my life for so many years because of the fear of the unknown, of not trusting that lasting change could even be possible. Again, it was through Donna's unique methods that I finally pushed through to the other side where love and joy are my constant companions.

During class she presented us with an "Opportunity for Transformation," in which we would journal about a question/prompt she provided. Her question hit me over the head like a cement block ... ouch!

If I am unwilling to transform my life what will it look like in five years?

My sweet heart sank as I journaled, "Well shit! I don't want to be sitting here cleaning the house, cooking the food, mowing the yard, playing wife! There's way too much fun to be had! It will be more of the same; boring, ho-hum, feeling stuck, sad, and obligated to others. I am fully aware that this is not my soul's highest purpose for my life! My rote routines of shopping, playing small, and running away will continue. When you always do what you've always done, you always get what you always got! WOW!!! Your choice, Abbi, you get to choose. Enough said!"

Out of the many journaling prompts I would receive, that was one of the most life-changing and motivating. It was high time this sweet, amazing woman I knew myself to be, got the ball rolling and started living my dreams so I could meet each day, excited to make it my best day ever. I created my own prompt: I have been playing it safe long enough, what would it take to start living the life I love?

In my coaching with Donna, I've learned that it takes willingness and courage to make lasting changes so I can strive for my best life. It includes being prepared to take deep dives within my Being to get in touch with my Soul's highest longings, desires and purpose for being here on this earth. It requires trusting the Divine unknown, embracing uncertainty, the willingness to move forward anyway; of pushing beyond the boundaries of fear, inch by inch. It requires eagerness for trying something new and different to see what grows from each experience. It's trial and error, but what have I got to lose? The answer is, a lot less than what I would miss by doing nothing.

Making myself a priority is always about the relationship I have with myself. I now regularly ask myself things like: "Is the relationship I have with myself one of honesty, integrity, and commitment? Am I a big listener to myself and my ideas and desires? Am I willing to continually work to make the necessary changes that would allow for my highest good? Finally, do I have the "Me First!" mentality?"

Of course, this was not always easy for someone who for years had tended to the needs of my family and others, before my own. The turning point came when I allowed myself to envision the worst that could happen if I didn't make myself a priority: I would leave this earth unsatisfied because I had not fulfilled my soul's purpose. Right then and there, I made a strong commitment to step into all of who I am, more and more each day!

Me First!
First thing in the morning!
Me First sprinkled throughout my day!
End my day with *Me First*!

CHAPTER 14

Embracing All of My Sweet Self

*"If you want to fly on the sky, you need to leave the earth.
If you want to move forward, you need to let go of the
past that drags you down."*

~Amit Ray

As we go through life, we all collect thorns that represent the "ouches" we perceive from living life and interacting with others. This is part of our human conditioning. As a sensitive person, I believe I have probably collected enough thorns to fill a rose garden! In his book *Unleashed,* Michael Singer paints a crystal-clear picture of what our lives are like when we have a bunch of thorns (hurts and resentments) embedded in us. He shared that we have two choices: we can use all kinds of "protection devices" that may keep the thorns from irritating us, but lead to a contracted life, or we can choose to do the work to pluck out the thorns, thus freeing ourselves from them forever. Either way, it's painful and takes a diligent effort.

While there are many ways to distract ourselves from feeling the thorns within, the protection device that worked most effectively for me was busy-ness – I was overly busy doing house and yard work, overly busy exercising, shopping, overly busy volunteering, and overly busy in my mom role. I developed these unconscious behaviors to avoid coming face to face with me; to avoid checking in to see how I was feeling because I thought my pain was too great a burden for me to bear.

It was only when the pain turned into misery that I finally decided to take an honest look at myself. Sometimes it takes getting to that point before we realize that freeing ourselves from all the "ouches" stuck inside can't be any worse than the agony of trying to keep the thorns protected.

It must be said that removing the thorns that have festered and been embedded in us for most of our lives is not for the faint of heart. It takes courage, diligence, stamina, and commitment. Through the process, I have learned the truth of what my sweet sister Heidi told me: that I am way more resilient than I ever thought possible. Consciousness is also a requirement, as many of our thorns have been buried so deep that we are not even aware of their existence. Unless I was willing to wake up to the present moment and see what my disturbances were, the thorns were only going to continue to bother and irritate me and I would be clueless as to why I felt so irritated. For heaven sakes, my nickname used to be "Crabby-Abbi" because I would act so feisty!

Singer also points out that we free ourselves by finding ourselves, and that we are not the pain we feel. That pain is simply stored energy from the past that is being released by the heart and in the process generates all kinds of crazy-making thoughts. He says we are the one who notices these thoughts therefore we can choose to stop entertaining them and become the silent observer instead.

When I feel a disturbance, which is usually a judgment, I can simply notice that I notice. Singer illustrates it in this way; "I am the subject, the one who sees what is happening in my mind. I am looking at an object (disturbance); it is something I feel but it is not me." (If it isn't me then I am free to be the best version of myself which is my pure loving essence.) These disturbances are just like a young child pulling on the mother's sleeve, asking to be seen, asking for kind attention.

Singer stated, "The one who notices is already free. If you want to be free of these energies, you must allow them to pass through you instead of hiding them inside of you."

He acknowledged that we all have these energies going on inside us, and we each have a sensitive part within us. He calls us to simply watch that sensitive part, feel the disturbances, and just embrace them as part of our humanness. When we can maintain our center as the loving Being, we can learn to appreciate and respect even the most difficult experiences.

I have cultivated a sacred practice where I sit with myself and allow my Being to feel the flow of energy from within, that I know as Spirit. When I tap into this energy I can more easily be with my disturbances and just watch them pass on through. I don't have to do anything about them except gently notice, give them some kind attention, and then allow Spirit to pour the self-love and self-compassion from a huge crystal pitcher inside my body. This builds the spiritual muscle, and the more I practice it the stronger the spiritual presence is within me. It frees me to live a heart-centered life.

It's taken a lifetime to learn to free myself from the pain of all the thorns I took on, and the feelings of guilt and shame were the biggest challenges. As a young girl I got scolded often, with an adult's pointer finger shaking in my face saying, "Shame on you, Abbi! You shouldn't have done that; you are a bad girl!" The guilt, I remember, felt overpowering. Over time the feeling of shame – the sense that I had not only done wrong but *was* wrong – seeped deep into every fiber of my being. It eventually eroded my somewhat healthy sense of self and I settled into living my life as the smallness of me rather than shining my light for all to see. Living from a place of guilt and shame created a set of thoughts and beliefs that perpetuated more of the same. It flavored how I operated in many aspects of my life.

From this place of guilt and shame, I developed the disease of pleasing others, which at the time felt like a wonderful coping mechanism. I convinced myself that if I could please other people then I could somehow free myself from the bondage of the deep shame and disgust I held for myself. It worked well for much of my adult life, until the day I woke up and realized the only person I ever needed to please was sweet, precious me. I was sick and tired of putting the needs of others before my own. I felt empty and neglected. That was a momentous space in time! Soon after that awareness my life started to shift and change in magnificent ways that I previously wouldn't have thought possible.

Learning the practice of *Compassionate Self-Forgiveness* as prescribed by Ron and Mary Hulinek, the founders of Spiritual Psychology, has been the master key to unlocking all the pain and suffering I have endured. The process allows me to find my way back to the pure essence of love that I am. Permitting myself to release the thorns, dissolves the judgments, which in turn brings healing to the hurt places. Poet Rupi Kaur suggests: "To heal you have to get to the root of the wound and kiss it all the way up."

I grew up with an extremely judgmental father and learned to internalize those judgments, which I then used as a way to "get through life." The practice of self-forgiveness has played a monumental role in my freedom. I came to terms with the notion that underneath the emotional upset or the disturbances were judgments that in reality had nothing to do with me being a good or bad person. *As humans, we are all doing the best we can.* That statement has held great significance for me in learning to neutralize and release judgments so I can move forward to self-acceptance and more of my loving essence.

When we have compassion for ourselves, when we can be with ourselves in a loving way when we are suffering, we can unlock that suffering. The *Compassionate Self-Forgiveness* process I use goes like this; "I forgive myself for judging myself as *wrong*. The truth is I am a Divine Being, and I am doing the best I can." Another example that gets to the heart of all the mistruths is: "I forgive myself for judging myself for buying into the misunderstanding *that I was responsible for her sadness.* The truth is *I did the very best I could when I was a child."*

This process then leads to acceptance of whatever is right here, right now. I don't have to label it as good or bad, just trust that it is exactly what my soul needs for healing. I believe we are presented with experiences and opportunities that are perfect for our human growth and evolution. Of course, this leads us to the pure loving essence of our empowered authentic self, and that is my goal, always.

Along with the forgiveness practice, I recently explored a very powerful process called *Family Constellations* developed by Bert Hellinger. A book by Mark Wolynn, *It Didn't Start with You,* is helpful in learning how to return to a state of wholeness. It was recommended to me so I could heal the broken bond I had with my dear sweet momma. Tina Paterson, a coach trained in this work, facilitated this process for me in the most compassionate, provocative manner.

Scientific research supports that traumatic experiences can be passed down through generations and show up in our bodies as depression, anxiety, chronic pain, phobias, and obsessive thoughts. Even if the person who suffered the original trauma has died or their story is forgotten or silenced, memory and feelings can live on in the bodies of the following generations.

Speaking from experience, this process goes way beyond anything cognitive behavior therapies could do for one's healing and evolution. It's one thing to talk about an issue, but true freedom came when I allowed myself to release and transcend old ancestral patterns.

As Wolynn says, "These emotional legacies are often hidden and encoded in everything from gene expression to everyday language and can play a huge role in our emotional and physical health."

Wolynn, a pioneer in the inherited family trauma field, also developed a pragmatic and prescriptive guide called the *Core Language Approach.* He utilizes diagnostic self-inventories to provide a way to uncover the fear and anxiety conveyed through everyday words, behaviors, and physical symptoms. Then an extended family tree or genogram is created from the experiences of past generations. The use of visualization, active imagination, and direct dialogue create pathways to reconnect, integrate, and reclaim life and health.

For me, the *core complaint* or the deepest issue I desired to heal was, "Not feeling loved by my mother." Then I was asked to develop *core descriptors* for both of my parents.

I described my mother as; "Always busy and distracted and unable to connect with me on a close emotional level."

I described my father as; "Harsh, reckless, and very critical of the entire family."

Then I shared what I blamed my parents for: "I blame my mother for not giving me what I needed to feel loved and emotionally connected." I blame my father for not keeping me safe, protected, and loved."

Finally, I was asked to develop a *core sentence,* which was: "My worst fear is that I am unlovable and will be left alone to die."

The core sentence not only guided me to the source of my fear, but it also connected me to the feelings of unresolved family trauma still living in my body. After gathering the information, the coach was able to take those statements and develop the genogram. She then spoke to me about the trauma in ways that allowed me to acknowledge it, see it didn't belong to me, and release it so transformation could occur.

Now, when I hear that voice that says, "Don't leave me!" I know how to process it.

As a young girl, I watched "Lassie," and in every episode, Lassie got lost and separated from her owner. I would get so sad and scared I would have to leave the room because I couldn't handle the thought of her being separated from the one who loved and cared for her. It felt so real for me. The same thing happened with the song, "Where has my Little Dog Gone?" As a child we used to sing around the piano while my mom played our favorite songs, and whenever one of my sisters chose that song I would run from the room, my hands clamped over my ears. It tapped right into the part of me that felt abandoned and so alone.

While practicing the *Core Language Approach* it became evident to me that the trauma I had experienced had possibly been perceived by my parents when they were children. My father had been ignored by his parents when he was a kid, then sent away for his high school years. At nineteen, his own dreams fell by the wayside when he had to pick up the pieces at the farm after his father's death.

Mom possibly fled to the farm because she was desperate to escape life with her own cold-hearted mother. Thus, each brought to the marriage their unresolved hurts, and just three years later found themselves the parents of three daughters.

It makes sense to me that I inherited those same feelings of being unlovable, and the fear of being left alone. Research shows we absorb our parents' suffering – even when the cause of that suffering occurred before we were born – and that it will call out for healing until we find a way to resolve it. I found it essential to make peace with my parents, as this would not only bring peace to me but allow for harmony to spread to the next generations of my family. Once we heal our unresolved issues it positively affects those closest to us.

After I worked through the entire process of healing the broken bond with my mom, I was given several supportive statements to repeat six times a day for a couple of weeks. This would allow the healing to integrate into healthier thought patterns that I hold with my mother. My statements were as follows: "I am with you. I've got this. I will breathe with you until you feel seen and heard. I will breathe with you until you feel safe. I will breathe with you until we are one. I will breathe with you until we are integrated as one."

This process was powerfully transformative and has allowed me to reclaim the love I have for my mother. It taught me that my mother loved me in the way she knew how, though not necessarily the way I thought I wanted and needed to be loved. It reminded me that her pure essence is love, as is mine, so how could our relationship be anything less?

I was also able to transmute the idea that someone other than myself was responsible for loving and caring for me. Once I became aware that it was up to me, I was one hundred percent free to love myself and others unconditionally. Holding others responsible for my welfare was never any fun for me or them. Raymond Russ suggests, "Maybe loneliness is a lesson in self-love. Maybe that broken heart is the beginning of something far better and greater."

The foundation was laid for me to open up completely to the Divine, precious, sweet human that I am. Growing and cultivating the seeds of self-love, is an ongoing practice that I will embrace for the entirety of my days on this earth. Throughout all the work I've done, the most profound realization has been that when I deeply cultivate my love of self, I feel connected to Spirit and I am free to live in my place of loving. From that loving place I am free to grow, expand, and experience so much more of all the infinite possibilities life has to offer!

Author and spiritual teacher Matt Kahn says, "In self-love, you don't need the agreement of others to set yourself free or anyone's permission to be as you wish."

As a Divine Being whose essence is pure love, I rediscovered that I already have everything inside of me to embody self-love. As I stated earlier, life got in the way and I strayed far away from my true self. Coming home to all of me is allowing me to see myself as the authentic, empowered, loving woman that I am. I tearfully express my joy and gratitude for this understanding daily!

When I was young I quickly learned to loathe the word "selfish" and I felt a great deal of shame when a family member accused me of being so. As I stated earlier, it was from this place that I fell into the trap of people pleasing, hoping to relieve the burden of shame I carried around. Eventually, I learned that when I focused solely on pleasing others, I couldn't be the full expression of my true self.

The word "self" is derived from the Dutch *zelf* and the German *selbe* and means, "one's person." The meaning of the suffix *-ish* is the "nature or character of." Selfish, therefore, means "I'm embodying the nature of my own self." I intend to always be true to myself so I can be the full expression of me. What rings true for me is that by first having genuine love, care and concern for myself, I can then genuinely love and care for others.

My religious upbringing taught me that I was to put God first before all. What I've since learned is that the spirit of God lives within my being and together we are the co-creators of my life. The essence of that spirit is love; therefore, love is not something I have to get from anyone or anything, it is who I am.

The practice of Compassionate Self-Forgiveness was and will continue to be a vital practice that has allowed me to remove the thorns and release the less-than-loving emotions that want to be released from my sweet body, so I can move forward into more of my loving. Self-forgiveness is acceptance in action.

For years, I stayed patient and curious around the question, "What does self-love look like in my daily life?"

The Universe answered when I was ready, and that answer came in the form of a self-love assessment tool developed by Donna Bond. To take the self-love assessment go to; MeetingYourselfWithLove.com (I'm good either way, if it works or if it doesn't). It gave me what appears to be the "perfect recipe" for cooking up an abundance of self-love:

1. Become still, quiet and calm and tap into the Divine every day.
2. Develop my intuitive muscle by listening and asking questions about what my higher guidance has to say.

3. The most important relationship I have is with myself and I can embrace the idea that I am a Spiritual Being having a human experience.

4. To know that I am doing the best I can each moment of each day is loving and honoring my humanness.

5. Self-love is being okay with, "This is where I am right now," no matter what is going on in my life."

6. I voice my truths and express them in a way that is also in harmony with others.

7. I choose words that are kind and allow me to experience a higher level of love and acceptance.

8. When I authentically connect with myself and others I am in my loving place.

9. I am willing to be gentle with my ego especially during times of upset.

10. I honor and respect myself by taking time away to recenter myself in love.

11. I am consciously aware of negative self-talk so I can then return to my pure loving essence that I am.

12. In self-love, I set healthy boundaries with myself and others, and honor the commitments I make.

13. Everything is a learning opportunity and I honor all of my emotions without judgments.

As spiritual teacher Matt Khan says, "Each blessing of 'I love you' sends blessings of light to every heart on a quantum level. The most direct way to heal yourself and transform the planet occurs within the same heart-centered space."

CHAPTER 15

Who Do You Think You Are?

Look forward, not behind. Your best days are out in front of you.
Be focused and keep your dreams alive.

~Adedayo Olabamiji

"Whether you think you can or you think you can't, you're probably right." This quote from Henry Ford gets to the heart of how limiting beliefs can run our lives. When we become aware of our limiting beliefs and begin to investigate them, we can transform them from life-limiting to life-giving.

Once I committed to stepping fully into my true self, I found that there is a force at work within me that is greater than all the limiting beliefs I had allowed to define me. I realized that life had been truly happening for me, presenting me with endless opportunities to evolve and grow. I'm learning to embrace the idea that all it takes is a little willingness to see things differently and then let God do the rest.

I've had this recurring dream where I'm trying to drive my car up a very steep incline and I just never quite make it to the top. The symbolism of this was not lost on me. Often in life I would usually quit pursuing something new and different once my mind chatter began to replay the old tape: "You're not good enough, you aren't capable." I was allowing my doubts to steal my dreams and stop me mid-course without fulfilling my heart's desire. I am now exploring the life I would love to live instead.

Becoming aware of the role the ego has played in my life has also allowed me to begin transcending many of the limiting beliefs I've been carrying around for years. While studying with Donna I learned the ego is a necessary part of who I am – it contains my personality, the logical mind; it is where judgments and right and wrong thoughts are formulated. When we live by "right and wrong" perceptions it leads to the judgment of self and others and is the root of emotional suffering. The ego can also be demanding, urgent, loud, forceful, and insistent on being right. It wants everything to be perfect and thinks it knows what will happen in the future. The ego ultimately wants safety, security, comfort, and control. As the ego is here to stay, the question becomes so how do we integrate it with our Higher Self?

Donna explained that the other part of me is where my true essence resides; my intuition, Higher Self, or Soul. As I learn to tap into my intuition, my internal guidance system, I bring more balance, light, and expansiveness to my life. Intuition is always calm, grounded, and subtle. My Higher Self is patient and will wait until I get onboard; it has no agenda. Intuition comes from a loving place and is where my true, authentic self rests. It comes from a place of nonduality, in other words, where everything is neutral, with no right and wrong. It gives me moments of inspiration. When I choose to ignore the subtle voice it creates, I feel the imbalance somewhere inside my body. When the ego takes over, I begin to fight with myself, and I feel stressed. It takes trust to follow this guidance as it can be illogical, yet magical, and serendipitous. Uplifted feelings of joyfulness and aliveness magically drop in when I am in alignment with my Higher Self.

As a young girl I was quite skilled at creating fear stories and over the years I came to see them as the truth. Now I often laugh at how cute those stories are. Byron Katie, author and creator of "The Work," teaches us to investigate our thoughts by asking four simple questions: "Is it true? Can I absolutely know it is true? How do I feel when I believe this thought? and Who would I be without this thought?" After you do the inquiry on the particular thought, you look for a turnaround, which is about discovering an alternative, more peaceful thought. I am learning to "notice what I'm noticing" where my thoughts are concerned so I can dispel those mistruths.

I would much rather choose to be open to infinite possibilities than closed off by fear and worry. That said, in order to overcome fear, I must acknowledge it as a natural part of who I am. I keep moving forward through the discomfort, trusting in the process.

In transcending fear there may also be feelings of frustration that we can learn to become curious about. Donna taught me that to work through my fear stories I can ask, "Can I lay down my position? Can I let go of the way it was supposed to be? Can I tune into knowing that there is a divine natural order and harmony in life?"

From there I can move into acceptance and inquire: "What is here for me? What am I being shown? What can I learn?" I'm learning to tap into my Higher Divine Self and ask for help and guidance.

As I release the resistance, suffering diminishes, and acceptance arrives. Acceptance neutralizes any judgments I might have and allows me to come back to my true loving self where I can receive all the abundance the Universe has to offer.

My attitudes around fear are transforming and I am learning that I can view fear *as the farthest reach of the reality* I've known and been familiar with up until now. When I allow myself to dream and use my intuition to guide me, I can dream of a life beyond the border. I'm also learning to "do it anyway" when I am afraid.

We all have a spiritual nature to tap into so we can create whatever we desire for our lives. The source of who we are is always with us and it has to work *through* us to allow our dreams to come to fruition. We've been given the access point to our infinite mind through conscious awareness, and it is our job to utilize it. What we put our attention on the Universe hears as our intention. The Universe is sending messages all day long and I am learning to open up to receive them.

For example, if I see something I desire for myself in someone else I can interpret it as a sign that it will soon be coming to me by making a statement such as, "There it is! I'm getting closer to realizing this dream." I am patient and I know it is coming to me in some form, with perfect timing.

A sign that I wasn't open to receiving love came in the form of birthday cards from my dearest loved ones. I would open a card and read all the sweet things it was supposedly saying about me and not believe a word of it! Furthermore, I judged the person for giving me a card with words they didn't mean.

On my birthday my husband gave me a card that stated what a lucky guy he was to have me for his wife and what a great person I was.

I looked at him with tears in my eyes and said, "Why did you give me this card? These words aren't true about me!"

Not skipping a beat, he replied matter-of-factly, "When I go to pick out a card, I read five or six cards before I decide which one best describes how I feel about you."

Needless to say, I was shocked, and decided that it was another sign for me to begin loving myself so I could receive all the good the Universe was offering me.

I've lived in my comfort zone a good share of my adult years, and the view from this vantage point is that nothing too spectacular ever happens; life is pretty predictable, mundane, and quite boring. It was only after I stepped out in faith and curiosity that I began to become conscious of my potential and what was truly possible for me. "Who do I think I am to be living so large?" became "Why would I not choose to live large and in charge of the best life possible?" As the saying goes, "Ask and you shall receive," and why would it be different for me than anyone else?

Once I committed to living up to my full potential I could then start identifying more of my truth as a human being. The two words, "I Am" are synonymous with the Divine energy that is within all living things. *Conversations with God,* author Neale Donald Walsh states, "You are always connected to Source. Wherever you are, wherever you go, you are always connected to Divine Wisdom, Divine Intelligence, and Divine Love."

Our beliefs create our world, it's that simple. I can choose to put an end to thought patterns that no longer serve me, and begin creating thoughts that I love. "I AM" is one of the most powerful statements I can make, for whatever follows the I AM starts the creation of it. "I AM" is a one hundred percent pure statement of creation.

As pastor Joel Osteen says, "What follows the 'I AM' will always come looking for you."

As the co-creator of my reality, I've got to believe it to see it. I have to spend time putting my attention on it. What do I want to create in my life? I have unlimited power and creativity and my Inner Spirit knows this. Action matters, but the action alone is not enough! I am learning to walk the talk.

Of course, the ego will always want to hijack me and say, "That's a bunch of malarkey; you can't physically see it, so it's not real and you can't wish it into existence. That is what the ego does, and I fell prey to it most of my adult life; in fact, there were times when my ego was so strong and overpowering that I doubted whether there was a Higher Power at play in my life at all. It has been my daily practice of I Am statements that has helped me break this pattern. The key is to slow down and listen so I can "hear" the messages my Higher Self has been so patiently trying to deliver, then own them through the statements.

This is an example of how I use "I Am's" in my life: *"I am so happy and grateful now that I am living from my loving place. I am so happy and grateful now that I am aware of all the ways life is loving me. I am so happy and grateful now that I am aware of when I need to turn my thoughts around to create the joy and happiness of who I truly am. I am so happy and grateful now that I feel the love that surrounds me. I am so happy and grateful to share my love and joy with others. This or something better for the highest good of all. And so it is."*

In *Remembering the Light Within*, Ron and Mary Hulnick explain:

> Silence is a gateway to profound Peace. It is also a doorway to your Awakening and the revelation of your Authentic Self. To hear the deepest Wisdom of the Spiritual Heart, it is necessary to give yourself time and space for contemplation, reverie, and reflection. When you withhold the gift of Silence from yourself, you are effectively blocking access to the wellspring of Creativity within and the Wisdom, Inspiration, and Guidance of your Soul.

Heart-centered listening taught me how to tap into the power of the higher self, and to embody the love and support that are readily available. Implementing this very powerful practice to live the life I love takes affirming that I am Divine and knowing I am unlimited in what I desire to create for my life. I spend time every morning devoted to heart-centered listening, so I hear the messages Spirit has for me each new day!

CHAPTER 16

What Am I Waiting For?

*"You gain strength, courage, and confidence by every experience in
which you stop to look fear in the face. You must do the thing
which you think you cannot do."*

~Eleanor Roosevelt

A s I was listening to the "DreamBuilder" lesson by empowerment
specialist and coach, Mary Morrissey, I had a profound wakeup call
moment. Morrissey shared an analogy comparing our lives to an ocean.
"Each day," she said, "you get to decide if you are going to take a teaspoon
of water for the day, scoop up a bucket of water for the day, or dive in and
swim with all the wonderful possibilities the day has to offer."

I sat there for a minute, dumbfounded. *Oh, my goodness!* I thought, *I've only
been taking a teaspoon of water way too many of my days on this precious earth.*

I became curious about what else was possible for my life and I realized
the opportunities were there for the taking. I noticed a longing that had
been within me for years, and it had to do with my passion for connect-
ing with people and engaging in inspiring and uplifting conversations about
this miraculous life. I would love to speak publicly about my journey to my

Empowered self. I am working on a life coaching certification that includes the DreamBuilder curriculum so I can help people learn how to live a life they love at no matter what age, it's never too late! I am also learning how to deepen the relationships I have with my loved ones and to genuinely give and receive the endless supply of love that is available.

Was I going to choose to live my life by design, listening to the longing and discontent that Mary speaks of so I could create the adventures I wanted to experience, or would I continue living by default, just the same old stuff day after day? It didn't take me long to discover that my true self was ready and destined for more. I was ready to rise to the occasion to give life all I've got. No more taking only a teaspoon of water for my day, making sure I was comfortable and safe. I committed to becoming courageous, ready, and willing to dive into all the sweet possibilities this life has to offer.

Writing this book has helped me find that long-forgotten voice. It made me aware of how necessary I thought it was for me to play small in my family and to keep quiet, so I didn't upset the already unsteady apple cart. As I mentioned earlier, all families have a dynamic where each member plays a certain role in service to the whole. It can serve a family quite well, and when we realize those patterns no longer serve us, we get to change the role to one that allows us to function better. For me, this has meant taking an inventory of my patterns and limiting beliefs and being willing to discern whether or not it is part of my authentic, adult woman self.

I have had numerous great teachers and mentors throughout my life who have provided me with the gentle (and sometimes not so gentle) nudges to get going. I can finally say that I do believe in myself and I do have talents, passions and abilities to share with the world. I will forever be grateful that I could be a stay-at-home mom all those years and focus on my children's healthy development. I know I wasn't as available for them emotionally as I would have liked, but again I did the best I could. We all get to do better when we know better. All four are adults out in the world living their best lives and I love, honor and respect each one for their many talents and abilities they are utilizing and contributing to others.

I am preparing to launch my own well-being coaching business in the coming months, something just year ago I would not have entertained. Now I know I have the tools and resources I need to make it happen. It feels so wonderful to be my empowered, authentic self, living out my dreams. I have so much gratitude for the Universe, my ancestors, and my parents for giving me the gift of life. I will find the resources necessary to grow my business to the desired size and will have plenty of fun along the way. I look forward to writing a business plan, meeting new people and expressing my creative talents in ways that are a positive contribution to others.

A lifelong Midwesterner, I describe myself as a daisy in the middle of a cornfield. I have never enjoyed following the crowd, nor have I always been satisfied with the norm set by society. I am the creative expression of myself who desires to do life in my own, unique way. I am willing to share my loving self with others and be all of who I am regardless of what the norm is in our rural, farming community. I was created to blaze trails that allow me to let my brightest light shine! I have always been told to "bloom where I am planted," and I'm choosing to do exactly that. In my eyes, sometimes the gift lies in being different. In the words of poet Elizabeth Appell, "And the day came when the risk to remain tight in the bud was more painful than the risk it took to blossom." Life is way more exciting when you are free to be all of who you truly are without caring what other people think.

As I have watched my life come full circle, the significance of the "circle your wagons" concept taught me by my beloved grandmother has become more important than ever. Even though Grandmother Eunice wasn't biologically a Harrington, she certainly shared the values of her beloved husband, Wayne Harrington, in his quest for living his best life. I know I wouldn't be where I am today without the strength, will, and courage that is embedded in my family's heritage.

Part of that heritage includes the embodiment of the strong sense of equality and fairness for all of humanity possessed by the women in my family. The potential for greatness is stronger whenever we come together to love and support our families, friends and our communities. I see this daily in my sisters, with whom I share a bond that cannot be broken. We have stood by each other through all of life's many challenges and we all know we are just a phone call away. I have the highest regard, respect and honor for each one of them, who brings her own set of gifts, talents and abilities to create the unbreakable whole.

As Heidi so eloquently says; "The women in our family have empowered my heart to do good for all."

In this book, I share my own words of wisdom, my own legacy of love for my entire family who is as precious as gold to me. It is also an homage to the very honorable, empowered women – my grandmothers, mother, sisters and their daughters – who keep the family nurtured and held in love. Looking back at the women in generations past it is evident that without the Harrington women standing so strong our namesake wouldn't have survived as long as it has. I also have no doubt the Harrington women in the generations to come will thrive and be actively involved in making this planet a better place for all of humankind. When women take over the world and care for all of humanity with love, we will then be able to embody the true loving essence that we all are. I'm ready for the revolution. Are you?

Acknowledgments

To my youngest son, Cameron, whose repeated encouragement to "Keep writing, Mom," inspired me to persevere through the many long days at home during the pandemic. Cam is my greatest spiritual teacher and has the grit and determination to beautifully navigate this world as a young Black man. He has my highest respect and honor and I know he will have the most amazing life!

To my oldest sister, Terri, for always being my cheerleader, excited to hear what I had been writing about lately.

To Lois Meyer, a respected English teacher whose commonsensical methods helped my language-impaired son find success in the public school system. She so generously agreed to be the first to read my rough draft and give me her honest feedback and encouraged me to publish my story.

I acknowledge myself for having the tenacity to keep going when I had moments of doubt and uncertainty, especially toward the end. And, finally, to my Higher Power, whose presence is within me, always.

Author Bio

Abbi K. Harrington is an author, former school teacher, fifth-generation farmer and certified life coach. A lover of all living things, she resides on the prairie and embraces the changing seasons of nature, and of life. One of the greatest joys of her life has been raising her four sons and observing their beautiful souls navigate life in their own unique ways. Abbi considers herself a social activist and was once arrested in front of the White House for civil disobedience. She and her husband are partners in their farming operation in the heart of America, which is her husband's deep passion. Abbi's hobbies include spending time in nature, sharing in her grandchildren and their families lives, hiking, traveling, and gardening. She is committed to self-love, awakening to her empowered, authentic self and is so grateful for the work of Spiritual Psychology that guides her heart and soul in such a beautiful way.

Bibliography

Remembering the Light Within; A Course in Soul-Centered Living by Ronald Hulnick, Ph.D., Mary Hulnick, Ph.D., 2017

It Didn't Start with You; How Inherited Family Trauma Shapes Who We Are and How to End the Cycle, by Mark Wolynn, 2016

The Untethered Soul; The Journey Beyond Yourself by Michael A. Singer, 2007

Trespassing Across America; One Man's Epic, Never Done Before, and Sort of Illegal Hike Across the Heartland, by Ken Ilgunas, 2016

Do You Feel Authentically Empowered? By Donna Bond, M.A., Blog Post, 2019

Aurora; A Wartime Love Story by Marie Kramer, 1998

funny — I don't remember being bigger than you guys...

Bishop and Mrs. Noah W. Moore gave a reception at their home Monday for the 800 delegates to the Nebraska Conference of United Methodist Church. Attending were (foreground, from left) **Mrs. C. W. Mead** of Omaha, **Bishop Moore**, **Mrs. Wayne Harrington** of Omaha and **Mrs. Moore.**

Midlands Homes
Editorials, Opinions

Sunday World-Herald

Real Estate
Want Ads

OMAHA, NEBRASKA, JUNE 23, 1968

SECTION F—SIXTEEN PAGES.

Where Sofa Can't Reach The Floor

Above—Looking a bit Oriental or like an alpine lodge, Harrington home rises out of the flatness of Nebraska.

Right—Benches instead of chairs used at breakfast table.

Left—Bookshelves slant in library. This might have been one of Mr. Harrington's few goofs.

Below—Mrs. Harrington reads as daughter Jenni swings. Fireplace to left rusting and may someday nearly match carpeted walls.

Benedict, Neb.—Several surprises await any one stepping inside the Tom Harrington home for the first time. Mr. Harrington lives six miles west of Benedict, which is on Highway 81 eight miles north of York, Neb.

Most visitors see the living room and its stone floor first. Orange carpeting climbs the walls in the living room and in some other rooms, carpeting covers bureaus and chests.

Mr. Harrington suggested some things to the decorator. Most worked out to his liking—a swinging sofa for instance—but in a few areas "I goofed," Mr. Harrington said.

The swinging sofa is in the living room near the suspended fireplace. It's an ordinary sofa with the legs sawed off and chains down into its arms so it can sway freely.

That wall-climbing carpet covers most of the light switches. "You ought to see them try turning on the lights," Mr. Harrington said of first-time visitors.

The house is patterned after the ski lodges of Colorado. Mr. Harrington said, and it was designed by Dewey Deuring of Colorado Springs.

This is appropriate, Mr. and Mrs. Harrington ski frequently. Seventy people have sat in the living room with a fire going in the rusting fireplace and watched ski movies.

A visitor has a rough time taking his eyes or mind off the living room but there are other surprises elsewhere. The slanting book shelves in the library, for instance, which Mr. Harrington now says might have been an error. "I had the idea bookends would be needed if the shelves weren't slanted," he said.

But the sunken bathtub in the master bedroom was no mistake. The water doesn't merely dribble from a faucet. It cascades in a waterfall effect.

The orange wall carpet was no mere whim, however. Designer Edward Morrow of Lincoln suggested it. Otherwise, he said, the house would be not big echo chamber as the family of six walked across the stone floor.

And carpet the walls in the breakfast room on the east side of the house. The family sits on benches here.

The master bedroom is on the east side of this large house. Bedrooms for the Harrington girls, Yael, 17; Heidi, 10; Abbi, 8, and Jenni, 4, are on the west side. The pool-sized kitchen, bathrooms, utility and other rooms complete the west and west sides of the structure.

The south end of the living room is a wall of glass. Curved tables sit in each corner at the side of the glass. These can be used separately or merged into a large dining table. Drapes, again in orange, can be pulled across the glass.

Mr. Harrington operates a cattle feeding lot near by. He is seldom more than a few hundred feet away from his unusual home.

CONTEMPORARY DESIGN—The long, low ranch-style home of Karen and Tom Harrington can be found five miles southeast of Polk. Built eight years ago, the home was designed by a Colorado architect.

It's Not Your Average Farm Home

By JAN WARE

POLK — Living in a small farmhouse with many rooms helped pave the way for the open design of the home of Tom and Karen Harrington.

The Harringtons farm five miles south of Polk and moved into their contemporary home eight years ago. Their former home is located just over the hill.

"The space in our other house was limited," Mrs. Harrington said. "And, like most farm homes built in that era, it was beginning to need remodeling."

The search for a design for a new home began with a friend's brother who is an architect. The Colorado Springs architect designed most of the home and custom designed the home's central fireplace and some doors. Mrs. Harrington said her husband also did a lot of the planning.

One special addition was his plan for slanted bookshelves in the family den. She said the slanted shelves eliminated the need for bookends.

The many small rooms in their old home resulted in an open spacious living-dining area. The central portion of the home is devoted to a large sunny multi-purpose room with a south window wall and beamed ceiling. Here is a hanging couch, musical center, dining area and the fireplace.

The Harringtons have four daughters, Terri, 17; Heidi, 16; Abbi, 15, and Jenni, 11. When planning their new home, Mrs. Harrington said they tried to anticipate the needs of their growing children and report they have not had many problems. The girls share living quarters and the arrangement seems to be working, Mrs. Harrington said.

Home of the Week

FREE-STANDING FIREPLACE—A central feature of the Harringtons' wide-open family living room is this ceiling-high fireplace. Mrs. Harrington said the fireplace gets quite a bit of

Saturday, December 7, 1974   Grand Island (Neb.) Daily Independent   1

COME SWING WITH ME—Decorated predominately in orange, this
hanging couch is one focal point of the living room.

FAMILY DEN—Mrs. Harrington said her husband planned the
_____ den so that bookends would be un-_____

CPSIA information can be obtained
at www.ICGtesting.com
Printed in the USA
FSHW020337051021
85183FS